BOYD COUNTY

DEC 0 6 2019

PUBLIC LIBRARY

D0848176

# THE MEXICAN KETO COOKBOOK

# THE MEXICAN KETO COOKBOOK

### AUTHENTIC, BIG-FLAVOR RECIPES
### FOR HEALTH AND LONGEVITY

## TORIE BORRELLI

### PHOTOGRAPHS BY ERIC WOLFINGER

Ten Speed Press
California | New York

# CONTENTS

# FOREWORD

*The Mexican Keto Cookbook* is an excellent guide for those people who feel stuck in their health journeys. All too often as a doctor, I see people who are sluggish, fatigued, irritable, and have trouble losing weight. They are not sure what to eat or how to prepare healthful food, at an affordable cost, that feeds their entire family.

Torie's book offers practical solutions for nourishing and nutrient-dense foods that complement preventative living. Familiar Mexican recipes often incorporate grains and corn, which are needlessly sprayed with herbicides, stripping them of vital nutrients before being sold to the public. Conventional dairy and factory-farmed meats have made it difficult for consumers to find clean and nutritious meal options. For years, the United States has relied on quick diet fixes, including low-fat fads, which use processed sugar, artificial sweeteners, high sodium, or "natural flavors" to trick our taste buds into feeling satisfied without the nutrients necessary to nourish our bodies. And there has been a surge in chronic disease leading to symptoms such as obesity; nearly 75 percent of American men and 60 percent of American women are considered overweight. Metabolic syndrome, which encompasses diabetes, heart disease, and high cholesterol, has skyrocketed and is a leading cause of blindness, kidney disease, heart attack, and inflammation. Unfortunately, there is a widespread "pill for every ill" mentality in healthcare when the focus should be more on what we are or, for that matter, are not eating. Health begins at the end of our forks. Food is medicine.

One of the first questions I ask every patient is, "What is your diet like?" It is a topic that needs to be discussed more in healthcare, but unfortunately there is so much misinformation out there that even doctors, dietitians, and other practitioners are confused. Over the years, the public has been taught that low-fat is healthful, eggs have too much cholesterol, meat is carcinogenic, grains are healthful, and fat makes us fat. Herbicides, pesticides, fillers, additives, and stabilizers create inflammation in the human body. The truth is that highly processed, commercial foods in any form are unhealthful and inflammatory.

Our ancestors did not eat a diet containing much grain at all, yet today we rely on breads and pastas with nearly every meal! What we put in our bodies is essential to healing any chronic health condition. We need to be mindful of what we choose to consume, and for that reason, eating organic and simple is paramount to healing. Multiple studies are now showing that the pesticide Roundup Ready, or glyphosate, can disrupt our microbiome. We also now know that glyphosate affects the entire food system, from the earth, air, and water all the way up to humans. Genetically modified food (mainly corn, soy, and sugar) is treated with glyphosate, which creates issues when we consume it. Factory-farmed meats are inflammatory due to the inhumane conditions, growth hormones, and antibiotics that are used on the animals. These antibiotics and hormones affect us when we eat these animals. However, when you seek out pasture-raised, organic, or wild-caught quality meats and seafood, you remove the chemicals and grain-based diets those animals would otherwise be consuming.

Eating as our ancestors did puts the emphasis on whole foods with adequate proteins, little sugar, and lots of high-quality fats, from coconuts to olive oil. For many, a keto diet reduces inflammation, which is a leading cause of puffiness, weight gain, and irritability and is a root cause in so many chronic health problems, like diabetes and heart disease. In fact, I would wager to say inflammation is *the* root cause.

By following Torie's carefully crafted recipes, readers will not only be reducing puffiness and inflammation but they may be surprised to find that their brain fog and fatigue also lift. Keto diets have proven over and over that eating healthful fats do not make us fat. They are the key to putting the body into a state of ketosis, where energy can be made more efficiently from stored fat, which provides the brain with a steady, sustainable supply of fuel. It is the key to quick energy. In this book, Torie has done a fabulous job at educating her audience to the benefits of a well-rounded and sustainable keto diet. She is a leader in her approach with the science to back it up. I highly recommend this book for anyone that feels called to take a deeper look at the foods they eat and the implications this has on the mind, body, and soul. The keto diet has aided in healing so many along their chronic health journeys and is testament to the power of food. Let this book inspire you to become the healthiest version of you.

—Jessica Peatross: board certified MD in internal medicine;
  Gerson practitioner

# INTRODUCTION

## MY JOURNEY TO HEALTH

I discovered the keto-focused, anti-inflammatory lifestyle after struggling with my health for twenty-five years. When I was sixteen, I was diagnosed with celiac disease, Hashimoto's thyroiditis, and irritable bowel syndrome (or IBS), which I thankfully do not have today. While my daily work as an integrative holistic nutritionist includes helping people with everything from weight loss to diabetes, I have faced my own set of health issues over the years. About four years ago, I experienced a radical shift in my personal health that has led me to writing this book today.

My journey to finding health through nutrition has been an incredibly transformative one. I spent years trying the newest fad diets, every health trend under the sun, and the most punishing cleanses before I found something that worked for me. My goal for this book is to cut through all the confusing, conflicting health information and tell you everything you need to nourish your body. Cooking healthy meals with the right ingredients should be fun and inspiring—not a chore or intimidating.

Transitioning to a high-fat lifestyle has been one of the most impactful changes in my life. Before this, I was constantly "stabilizing my blood sugar" by eating every couple of hours to relieve my hanger. Switching to a high-fat ketogenic diet cleared my brain fog, energized me, and eliminated hunger pangs and mood swings from my life. Fat doesn't make you fat; it makes you thrive. After applying these principles to my own life and seeing dramatic changes, I started to implement them with my clients, friends, and anyone who wanted to let me guide them.

## THE HEALING TRANSITION

Before I launched my brand, The Vida Well, in 2016, I worked closely with leading naturopaths, chiropractors, acupuncturists, and local San Diego doctors. I helped develop personalized programs for their patients combating everything from daily concerns such as fatigue and skin issues to widespread chronic illnesses such as diabetes, heart disease, and obesity. This work inspired me to create The Vida Well, a wellness and education brand rooted in health and nutrition. I created this platform to open people's worlds by helping them take a preventative approach to living, which essentially means not waiting until sickness strikes in order to change habits. My work consists of meeting one-on-one with clients, corporate consulting, and teaching around the world.

The knowledge I had, along with the direct access to some of San Diego's best practitioners, helped me give patients the tools to change their lives through diet. And with this book, I can help so many more people than I would ever be able to on a one-on-one basis.

Throughout my work with thousands of clients, one thing has made itself clear to me: people are confused. There is an overwhelming amount of misinformation out there when it comes to what we should be eating. My clients will often share, with increasing exasperation and frustration, things they read online. They're hesitant to eat fat because they believe it will clog their arteries, and they're worried that skipping breakfast or snacks will cause a drop in blood sugar.

This book will dispel all the ambiguity by breaking down the science of nutrition into easily digestible information and giving you clear solutions to help eliminate sugar and reduce carbohydrates in your diet. Everyone I have worked with, no matter what symptoms they have, has benefited from this simple process.

I will not recommend anything in this book that I have not experimented with on myself. For so long, I felt like I tried everything from going gluten-free to using prescription medications. The major shift happened when my mind felt clear and I was satisfied after meals. With the keto diet, I have finally found something that not only works but is a tenable way to live.

## THE TRUTH

Chronic inflammatory diseases have never been more of a global problem than they are right now. Most of this is due to inflammation caused by poor nutritional habits, stress levels, sedentary lifestyles, abnormal sleep patterns, and environmental exposures. As our food becomes more sugar laden and processed, the number of people suffering with inflammation-based diseases such as diabetes, fatty liver disease, mental illnesses, digestive disorders, and even cancer continues to rise. The United States spends more on health care than any other country, yet our rates of disease are the highest in the world. Over half of the country is suffering from ailments that can be treated, managed, or even reversed through nutrition-based programs. My own experiences have inspired me to look for answers, but the positive change I see in my clients has turned it into my passion.

## THE SOLUTION

The good news is that this doesn't have to be the way. We can go back to a more intuitive way of eating and still live in the modern world. Pairing locally sourced and unprocessed foods with my simple high-fat, low-carb guidelines will transform the way your body functions and, with that, many aspects of your health.

I chose to focus on Mexican food for a couple reasons. I'm half Mexican and live in Mexico part-time, so Mexican cooking is like a first language to me. Traditional Mexican cuisine is high in healthy fats and proteins and lends itself well to a ketogenic diet. Finally, many of my clients have some sort of Mexican heritage like I do. Seeing people embrace their culinary roots firsthand and at the same time reverse their inflammation symptoms is one of the best parts of my job.

In researching the concept for this book, I started to explore the ways my great-grandparents ate and their relationship with food. What I discovered was that not too long ago, their diet closely resembled the one I have painstakingly discovered through trial and error. Slow-cooked meats, whole fish, and seasonal vegetables served with homemade salsas comprised the majority of their meals. You'll read more about the relationship between high-fat foods and Mexican cooking on page 8.

Everyone wants to lead healthier lives, but most are overwhelmed by either nutrition myths or inflammation ailments or both. Throughout this book, you will learn simple ways to prioritize your everyday health. This cookbook is your road map to wellness. You will learn that food reminiscent of *abuelita*'s cooking is healthier than any commercialized Mexican food you'll find today. These flavorful Mexican recipes will resemble what people ate before processed and fast foods became the norm in both Mexico and the United States.

My goal is to educate and empower by taking the traditional Mexican dishes I have always known and loved and updating them to optimize health in a delicious and enjoyable way. Each recipe will be accompanied by health tips, ingredient facts, and substitution ideas. I will also help you fill your kitchen cabinets with affordable and nutrient-dense staples. We want to create an enduring lifestyle change rather than a quick fix. It's time to become more connected with the food we put into our bodies and learn to listen to our bodies' signals.

Imagine a life where you have the energy to check things off your always growing to-do list, where you're sleeping through the night, not wearing as much makeup because your skin is now clear and glowing, where you're fitting into that favorite pair of jeans, and feeling like your best self. You slow down, listen, and understand the messages from your body.

Of course, there isn't a one-size-fits-all solution when it comes to nutrition. Everyone has their own taste preferences and health issues. Still, despite these distinctions, everybody can benefit from incorporating keto concepts into their life. All the research I have done, all my experiences working with people to better their nutrition, and my own personal journey with the keto diet have shown me that proactively reducing your inflammation leads to major health benefits. Imbalance is caused by inflammation. Just one imbalance creates oxidative stress in the body, which in turn creates mitochondrial dysfunction. Inflammation is something that every single one of us has, although the symptoms may present themselves in different ways.

These simple and straightforward recipes are low in carbs, high in healthy fats, and moderate in protein. This book uses the principles of the ketogenic diet (see page 16) and the pillars of Mexican heritage cuisine as the foundation for creating affordable and accessible meals that will reduce disease-causing inflammation in the body, speed up your metabolism, help shed those extra pounds, clear that brain fog, improve mental clarity, and balance your hormones.

It can be argued that everybody loves Mexican food—but that's not why I'm writing this book. People all over the world are sick and they are only getting sicker. There are so many conflicting opinions about what is healthy, and people fall into a mainstream-trending diet hole. They are afraid to include fat in their diets, opting for low-fat, high-sugar, and high-chemical products instead. Most people don't have easy access to nutrient-rich food, elite dieting fads, or posh cookbooks. My hope is that this book will start to bridge that chasm by bringing this information to people all over the world.

This book and my more than 85 Mexican-inspired recipes will be an extension of the work I do on a daily basis, in and out of the kitchen: identifying and combining the most nutrient-dense foods to create simple, delicious meals for you and your families. While most of these recipes are strictly ketogenic, I have found that keto-adapted, HFLC (high-fat, low-carb) cooking and eating is more sustainable and realistic for most people.

My Mexican American and Italian heritage has played a huge role in my journey, especially with my approach to recipe development. I grew up in a home that had a blend of cultural traditions where food was ultimately a key driver to our connectivity as a family, and that's the type of environment that shaped who I am today. The gathering around preparing and enjoying food brought us close; it's where we talked about the good times and the bad.

Sharing meals is the most universal tradition that humans have, and this sense of connection to others, past and present, is one of the many reasons I chose to focus on Mexican cooking. To me, Mexican dishes remind me of gathering together, of holidays spent with loved ones, and of home. Hopefully, this cookbook will inspire the same sense of connection in you.

My philosophy with food is simple—you should enjoy it. Life is too short, and there are too many delicious foods to waste time with diets that feel more like exercises in torture. Instead, embrace the pleasure. If you have space for a garden, I suggest trying to grow some food. Herbs, greens, and your favorite seasonal veggies are all you need to get started. If that's not realistic for you, buy food at farmers' markets or sign up for a community-supported agriculture (CSA) box. Try to be as local and sustainable as possible, and always strive to purchase food that is non-GMO and organic. Knowing where your ingredients come from and cooking them yourself creates a sense of well-being for you and the people you love.

I'm glad you're reading this book. You've made one small but important step toward changing the way you interact with food and your body. With just one step toward unlocking the secrets to your body's health, you have joined this wellness revolution. Wherever you are on your health journey, it is never too late to change your lifestyle, and I welcome you to the keto diet. Let's dig in.

## A CASE STUDY: INFLAMMATION-BASED DISEASE

Roberto B. is like most other thirty-seven-year-old Mexican immigrants living in the United States. He works long hours in construction; he cherishes his wife, Theresa's, cooking; and he drinks his Coca-Cola by the *medio litro*. When he started having trouble sleeping and felt body aches and pains, he chalked it up to the stress of making ends meet. After these symptoms became progressively worse, however, Theresa insisted that he see a doctor.

One week later, Dr. Peter Attia diagnosed Roberto with the worst case of type 2 diabetes and fatty liver disease he'd ever seen. The threat of losing a limb or worse was imminent. Alarmed at the progression of the disease, Dr. Attia called his mentor in Dubai, Dr. Naji Torbay, who suggested a prescription that was as simple as it was unrealistic. His recommendation? A three-month regimen of pills that cost about five hundred dollars per day. It was at this point that Dr. Attia decided to call me, asking for my help as both a translator and a nutritionist.

When Dr. Attia and I sat down with Roberto and Theresa to analyze his blood work, the severity of the situation began to set in. We didn't think this type of inflammation could be reversed through nutrition and inexpensive medication alone.

Dr. Attia asked if I could explain the seriousness of the situation in Spanish. Roberto needed to commit to this diet 100 percent—no cheating, no excuses—or he could potentially lose a limb. I struggled to keep the emotion out of it. Theresa asked me through tears if he was going to die.

Together, the doctor and I created a personalized program to reduce inflammation and mitochondrial dysfunction within Roberto's body. The plan had to be feasible for their lifestyle and tight budget. It consisted of shopping at three different grocery stores to find the highest-quality foods at the best prices; translating all medical and nutritional recommendations, recipe analysis, breakdowns of macronutrient percentages; and a tremendous amount of detailed note taking. In order to reverse this disease, three main health predictors had to drastically change; HbA1C (a diabetes marker), fasting glucose, and fasting insulin all needed to decrease significantly.

"Ordinarily, for a patient with this degree of disease . . . I would have opted for at least two drugs, metformin (cheap) and a DPP4 inhibitor (not cheap), and most doctors would have gone straight to insulin, as well. However, due to the patient's financial circumstances, we opted to only use metformin and dietary modification. . . . If we were going to fix him, it had to be through nutrition."
—Dr. Peter Attia

As I tracked Roberto's progress and his symptoms, I began to tweak the recipes and diet recommendations for him. I found that Himalayan salt combined with bouillon cubes helped with Roberto's dizziness—a symptom of his poor circulation. High-quality fats, like grass-fed butter, avocados, and pasture-raised lard, sated his cravings for sugar, which had developed over a lifetime of eating flour tortillas and drinking soda. I also found that certain supplements (such as magnesium and fish oil) relieved constipation, sleep problems, muscle aches, and soreness. I incorporated crucial ingredients and superfoods into dishes I knew he would want to eat.

After just three months of a high-fat, low-carb, anti-inflammatory meal plan, Roberto's symptoms began to dissipate. He had more energy, slept better, lost weight, and normalized his blood sugar. Finally, Roberto's body had started utilizing ketones. Roberto's labs changed exponentially in a short amount of time simply by sticking to this carefully crafted diet. This was crucial considering the urgency with which these changes needed to be made.

## SO WHY THE FOCUS ON HIGH-FAT MEXICAN FOOD?

Mexico has always been a second home to me, and I have a deeply rooted connection with the traditions and people of Mexico. I live part-time in southern Baja, in a small pueblo where I found inspiration for most of the recipes in this book. To me, Mexico is eating fresh seafood off a *ponga* (a Mexican fishing boat), cooking over a campfire on the beach, and enjoying life at a more *tranquillo* pace. As each year progresses, more of my friends are diagnosed with diseases, their children are overweight, and they still aren't sure what food they should be eating to optimize their health.

It's not just Mexico; the United States, with its quest for wellness through dieting and quick-fix trends, is sadly not getting healthier. Meanwhile, the French are eating foods rich in butter and animal fat without widespread disease and obesity. The Japanese enjoy a diet full of fatty fish and have been blessed with some of the longest lifespans on Earth. It's time to admit we are doing something wrong.

Like the French, the Japanese, and countless other cultures across the globe, Mexicans once enjoyed a rich land-and-ocean culture. What is commonly referred to as the milpa diet was an intuitive system of agriculture as well as a way of life throughout Mesoamerica. It's basically an ancient form of what we today refer to as organic farming. People grew several crops at once without artificial fertilizers and pesticides and rested the soil to keep it nutrient dense. One of the best things about the milpa diet is that it is sustainable at large volumes.

Crops such as maize, beans, squash, avocados, tomatoes, and chiles paired with small amounts of broth, animal fats, and wild fish and game provided everything a healthy body might need. Unfortunately, this all changed in 1994, when the United States, Canada, and Mexico entered into the North American Free Trade Agreement, aka NAFTA. While NAFTA helped Americans enjoy off-season crops such as corn, bananas, and pineapples year-round, sugar-laden, commercialized foods made their way across Mexico.

The sad truth is that a simple diet that was once rich with New World crops and wild game has been contaminated by America's overly processed food. Foods low in fiber, high in carbs, and packed with GMOs and sugars have become pillars of the Standard American Diet (SAD), spilling across the border into Mexico. As a result, our bodies have learned to rely on sugar, not fat.

Today, Mexicans are the largest consumer of carbonated drinks (also known as soda) on the planet, as well as the largest consumer of processed foods in Latin America. Chronic illnesses, like heart disease, obesity, and diabetes, are all growing at record rates. Mexico's market for diabetes devices is predicted to reach $1.209 billion by 2021. To say that the American health crisis is leaking across the border would be an understatement.

"Don't eat anything your great-grandmother wouldn't recognize as food." This is one of my favorite quotes from author, journalist, and activist Michael Pollan. And the question I ask of my clients or anyone who wants to know what to eat is, what would your great-grandmother be eating or cooking? I guarantee it wouldn't be that packaged junk or that microwavable meal. People always respond with the correct answers. I'm just not sure they make the connection as to why that food is so much better for them.

## GOOD FAT VERSUS BAD FAT

Every cell in our bodies is surrounded with a layer of fat. It is the primary source of energy. We cannot survive without fat! Fat slows the release of sugar into the blood. It helps us use minerals, vitamins, and protein in the body. Our brains are composed of 60 percent fat. That means fat equals optimal brain health, quicker cognition, and yes, the end of brain fog.

Fat, along with protein and carbohydrates, is a macronutrient. Its main role is to provide energy in the body. It's also in charge of health for every single cell in your body—that includes hair, skin, and nails. Fat helps you absorb fat-soluble nutrients and vitamins such as A, D, E, and K. Fat helps in regulating the immune system and helps reduce inflammation throughout the body.

Good, healthy fats play a huge role in balancing hormones, which, when imbalanced, contribute to low energy, weight issues, fertility issues, brain fog, and decreased metabolism. Fat balances insulin and spikes in glucose levels. My favorite part about fat is that it keeps you feeling full and satisfied, thanks to our amigo hormone leptin. Healthy fat is not going to clog your arteries, make you gain weight, or cause you to die of a heart attack. Fat is going to help you feel and look your very best.

## THE GOOD FATS TO EAT

- Organic, grass-fed, or pasture-raised beef, pork, poultry, and lamb
- Pastured and sugar-free bacon and bacon fat
- Wild-caught seafood

- Eggs (organic and pasture-raised)
- Grass-fed butter, ghee, tallow, and lard
- Dairy-milk products (organic, raw, whole, and full fat)
- Nuts (all except peanuts)
- Flax, hemp, pumpkin, sesame, and chia seeds
- Olives
- Olive oil (cold-pressed, extra-virgin)
- Avocados and avocado oil
- Sesame oil
- Coconut products, including MCT oil, butter, oil, flakes, and cream
- Algae oil

### SATURATED FATS

Poor saturated fat has had the most recent bashing thanks to flawed scientific studies. Most studies reported do not consider the high consumption of sugar and carbohydrates along with saturated fats. One example would be a store-bought salad dressing, like ranch or Thousand Island, loaded with sugars and inflammatory canola oil. This means the studies are skewed because of the processed carbohydrates.

Studies with low-carbohydrate diets, on the other hand, show improvements in blood glucose levels, cholesterol, weight loss, hormone support, insulin resistance, and heart health. These studies show that saturated fats have no negative effect on our health. These healthy saturated fats include butter, ghee, cacao butter, lard, high-fat dairy, coconut oil, and egg yolks. Keep in mind that quality does matter. Regular commercial butter, made from cows injected with hormones and antibiotics and who eat corn, soy, and grains, is not even comparable to grass-fed butter. Just like us, they are what they eat.

### MONOUNSATURATED FATS (MUFAs)

MUFAs are one of those fats that have always been supported by all sides for both anti-inflammatory properties and heart health. Think avocados, olive oil, and nuts. Okay, there are some people who still say that macadamia nuts have too much fat. I will eat theirs!

### ESSENTIAL FATTY ACIDS (EFAs)

We call them essential nutrients because we cannot make them in the body, so we must get them through our diets. They are required for the proper structure and function of every cell in the body and are necessary for our survival. They increase the absorption of vitamins and minerals and are optimal for health.

### OMEGA-6 TO OMEGA-3 RATIO

Understanding the omega-6 to omega-3 ratio is very crucial to our health. Both omega-6s and omega-3s are essential fatty acids that we cannot make on our own and must get from food.

Omega-3 fats are great for reducing inflammation; omega-6 may cause inflammation in the wrong amounts when not in balance with omega-3, especially if the omega-3 is low. The ideal ratio should be one to one (omega-6 to omega-3). We never had issues with our omega ratios before SAD foodways became the norm. These days the standard ratio can be upward of twenty-five to one. When your ratio is in balance, you are less likely to have inflammatory diseases.

### POLYUNSATURATED FATS (PUFAs)

PUFAs are controversial, but some are definitely good because they contain both omega-3s and omega-6s depending on their double bond. The reason they can also be negative is due to their omega-6 ratio, which, if you are eating omega-3s, you do not have to worry about. Always avoid refined vegetable oils such as canola, safflower, soybean, corn, and margarine.

### THE TRUTH ABOUT CHOLESTEROL

Let me start out by saying that cholesterol is not bad; it's actually good! Without cholesterol, we cannot live. It's a building block to our cell membranes. Our bodies produce about 75 percent of all the cholesterol within the body. It's regulated in the blood based on how much is needed. The remaining 25 percent of cholesterol comes from our diet. Dietary cholesterol does not raise blood cholesterol levels much, if at all. Crazy, right? So, get rid of those egg whites and swap them out for egg yolks. Cholesterol does not cause heart disease; inflammation does.

## THE FATS TO AVOID

- Commercially prepared baked goods, processed foods, and fast foods

- Conventional meats

- Conventional dairy

- All packaged foods containing hydrogenated and partially hydrogenated oils or the word "shortening"

- Industrially processed liquid oils such as soy, corn, safflower, cottonseed, and canola

- Fats and oils heated to very high temperatures (from cooking or processing)

- Margarine

- Trans fats

As people have reduced their intake of total fat consumption, many serious diseases have been steadily rising. The war on fat is so misguided and has created this health crisis we face today.

### WHAT ARE TRANS FATS?

Trans fats, aka partially hydrogenated oils, are unsaturated fats that are uncommon in nature but can be created artificially in a lab. They are made by forcing hydrogen atoms into liquid vegetable oils, which turns it into a solid, like margarine or Crisco. This gives them a longer shelf life, a more desirable texture, and flavor stability.

### WHAT'S WRONG WITH TRANS FATS?

Trans fats interfere with and block the healthy function of the essential fatty acids. Trans fats:

- Increase heart disease

- Increase sudden death from cardiac causes

- Lower "good" cholesterol HDL and raise "bad" cholesterol LDL

- Raise total serum cholesterol

- Impair artery function

- Increase risk for diabetes

- Negatively affect immune response

- Contribute to childhood asthma

In this book, I put my spin on traditional recipes by using fermented and pickled ingredients to add gut-healing probiotics and to help with the absorption of nutrients. I call for high-quality salt, like Himalayan, which brings about eighty-five different minerals to the body, and bone broths for collagen and organ meats for essential nutrients. I also throw in fats such as bone marrow, nuts, and MCT oils to help the body reduce inflammation and burn fat. Finally, I sneak in Mexican superfoods such as moringa, chia seeds, aloe, and chiles to add delicious taste as well as nutrient density.

It should go without saying that all processed foods should be avoided. Refinement processes such as homogenization, pasteurization, radiation, and so on actually destroy foods on a molecular level. These methods are highly toxic. By the time chemicals, preservatives, sugars, and other additives are pumped in, the final product hardly resembles real food.

I can't stress enough that healthy fats don't make you fat—it's quite the opposite. As we embark on this journey together, I will show you how to use healthy fats to optimize your health and well-being. *Vámanos!*

# HOW KETOSIS WORKS

The keto diet is also sometimes called the high-fat or high-fat, low-carb (HFLC) diet, and it is exactly that—high in good fat and low in carbs. Why the shorthand term *keto*? The term references a state of *ketosis*, which is a metabolic state where your body is burning fat instead of carbs for fuel.

For most of us, carbohydrates (which, when digested, become sugars called glucose) have been our primary source of fuel our whole lives. These days, our diets are filled with excess glucose. Some of the primary sources of glucose might even surprise you—the sugar found in fruit, for instance, is considered glucose.

How did we end up with so much misinformation? We are scared of fat, and this fear comes primarily from the food pyramid (now MyPlate). That ubiquitous chart that used to hang in many of our elementary school classrooms and cafeterias gave us incorrect information. The foundation of our diet according to the misguided food pyramid was supposed to be carbohydrates. Fats were at the tippy top of the diagram, and we were told to consume them sparingly. However, flipping the fat and carb categories would be a better starting point for all of us.

When we burn carbs or glucose for fuel, they give us a quick burst of energy. But it's not long before we crash, especially if we are dieting and already depriving ourselves in the name of health. I'm sure you've all experienced this at some point: the fatigue, brain fog, and hanger (stressful, right?).

Alternatively, when we burn fat for fuel, we experience a sustained energy with no crash. We are using ketones for energy. Ketones from fat (as opposed to glucose from carbs) are an energy source made by the body in the liver when glucose is scarce or unavailable. When blood sugar levels are low, our bodies enter the state of ketosis. The ketogenic diet is a return to humanity's natural source of energy before sugar and glucose became widely available; in long periods of fast, during famine, or in the cold winter months when carbohydrates weren't readily available, ketosis was a form of survival. Thankfully, our bodies can still adapt to utilizing fat for fuel under specific circumstances that include fasting, intense or long workouts, a carbohydrate-restricted diet, or a ketogenic diet.

The ketogenic diet is made up of:

• Fats (60 to 80 percent)

• Proteins (15 to 20 percent)

• Carbs (5 to 10 percent)

Eating processed foods high in carbs and sugar is a vicious cycle. As the carb boost fades, you are left hungry, irritable, and without the energy to properly fuel the rest of your day. The irony is that fat is actually a superior form of energy. All you have to do is see how great you feel once you are fat-adapted, meaning specific carb additions will not affect you as it could with someone who is suffering from diabetes, for instance.

The keto diet is so popular because it truly works. In addition to fat being a superior energy source, it also tells your body that you are satisfied, suppressing cravings for things such as sugar. It prevents brain fog, offering sustained mental focus and productivity. Research shows it can also help combat diseases such as diabetes, fatty liver disease, obesity, epilepsy, heart disease, stroke, Alzheimer's disease, and more. Ketosis regulates insulin sensitivity and balances glucose levels, which in turn reduces inflammation throughout the body, creating an environment that's inhospitable to disease.

### GLUCOSE VERSUS KETONES FOR FUEL

There are two main types of fuel sources for the body: glucose (sugar) and ketones (fat).

**GLUCOSE** is not the most efficient fuel source for our bodies because it creates insulin resistance, inflammation, and free radicals, which all trigger chronic diseases.

**KETONES** are the optimal fuel source our bodies (especially our brains) can use because they metabolize more quickly than does glucose and provide more energy. Ketones come from the metabolism of fat and are an essential source of energy within our cells. They help with weight loss, inflammation, energy, disease prevention, and mental performance.

## THE ROLE OF KETONES

Ketone levels can be measured by your breath, your blood, or your urine. In my practice, we check ketone levels in the body to see when a person is able to get into ketosis. While everyone can get into a state of ketosis, some people may take longer. Checking ketone levels is a great way for us to get a baseline and to track progress.

"Ketones are the preferred source of energy for your brain in general, but especially for those affected by diabetes, Alzheimer's, Parkinson's, and maybe even ALS, because in these diseases certain neurons have become insulin resistant or have lost the ability to efficiently utilize glucose, which causes the neurons to die off. When ketones are present, these neurons have a better chance of surviving and thriving."—Dr. Joseph Mercola

## MEN VERSUS WOMEN IN KETO

As annoying as it is (to me), men respond more quickly to keto. I personally have experienced this over the years with my husband (who eats whatever I feed him), and of course he can lose weight, change his blood glucose levels, and increase ketone production way quicker than I can. He can also fast longer than I can without even thinking of food (must be nice). In my practice, I have found that men do better on a strict keto diet than women because women tend to need more carbs due to hormones.

I notice around my menstrual cycle that I am moodier, and ketosis can throw off my hormone levels (especially the stress hormone called cortisol). In response, I increase my carb intake around my menstrual cycle. The female body needs good carbs for sleep and hormone regulation, but it *does* matter when you eat them and what type they are. Since my body is used to going in and out of ketosis, I am fat adapted. Of course, everyone is different, so I recommend doing some testing and listening to your bodies to find out which combination of fats, protein, and carbs is right for you.

I do not recommend keto for anyone suffering with gut issues, that cannot assimilate fat, has had gastric bypass or liver issues, is pregnant, or is breastfeeding. Please consult your doctors.

## IT IS PERSONAL

Is there a one-size-fits-all approach to going keto? The short answer is no. In fact, as I write this, we are shooting photos for this beautiful book, and my team is trying out the keto lifestyle. It has been so exciting to help each one of them in their personal situation understand how using keto (and fasting) will help them reach their health goals. Finger pricking upon rising and between meals helps me teach them where they are at and why they might be there. Depending on glucose levels, metabolism, activity level, stress, hormones, sleep—each person needs to fast at different times and has different outcomes (and that's okay!). Because the amount of carbs you need depends on so many factors, you must start listening to your body or consult an integrative practitioner.

## HOW TO SHIFT TO KETO

Try it out by doing strict keto for three months minimum. Most experts do not recommend staying in ketosis forever, and I agree. Depending on your goals and personal state of health, the time spent in ketosis varies.

1. Reduce carbs to 25 to 30 grams a day to start. Treat veggies like carbs now, and make sure they are slathered in fat. Aim to eat at least 4 cups of greens a day plus some brightly colored veggies. Remember all carbs are not created equal. You care only about net carbs, which are total carbohydrates subtracted by fiber. You want to be between 25 to 50 grams a day.

2. Read labels—there are tons of hidden sugars and carbs in things you would never expect.

3. Avoid all fruit for the first three months, after which you can have one cup of berries or half a piece of seasonal fruit for dessert or as a treat.

4. Avoid gluten and all grains.

5. Protein is very controversial because of *gluconeogenesis* (turning nonsugar compounds into sugar), but I have found with my clients that if they are not scared of overdoing the protein and fat, then they eat less carbs overall because they are more satisfied. (I do think food logging is good for specific situations, including obesity or extreme weight loss, metabolic conditions like diabetes, or extreme cognitive issues like Alzheimer's.)

6. Do not be scared to add your healthy fats. Most people do not get enough.

7. Increase electrolytes—no, not Gatorade, coconut water, or other sports drinks. Try water with Himalayan salt and lemon (see page 47). You can find trace mineral drops online.

## IDENTIFY KETONE PRODUCTION AT HOME

There are simple methods for identifying your ketone production without using a blood or urine test. I can get a fairly good read on whether a client has entered ketone production by asking a few questions. If you answer yes to any of these questions you are in ketosis.

- Do you have more energy after you eat?

- Do you have fewer sugar cravings and less hunger in general?

- Do you feel like you are more productive and focused?

- Are you thirsty?

You can also buy a ketone meter, which instantly checks blood ketones with a little prick of your finger. Aim for levels 0.5 to 6.0 mmol/L. Some meters can check blood glucose as well as blood ketones. I like a meter that does both. I also like a ketone strip you can pee on. I do recommend working with a practitioner (such as an integrative or functional doctor, or naturopath) to help you understand these numbers.

Once you're in a state of ketosis, you will feel like a million bucks; however, there may be an uncomfortable transition period in between. If your body has been reliant on sugar and carbs, you'll likely experience what is called the "keto flu," where you might feel worse before you start to feel better. The keto flu is a symptom of your body adjusting and usually occurs the first couple of days. The severity and length of the flu varies from person to person. Symptoms of the keto flu include stomach pain, irritability, cravings, headaches, nausea, and fatigue.

## THE WRONG WAY TO DO KETO

You should be using keto to optimize your health and not just as a weight-loss tool. One common misconception is that it's just about eating "fat" no matter the source. If you search for "keto" online, you'll see photos of bacon wrapped in cheese, the pork rinds from 7-Eleven dipped in food-dye-yellow cheese dip, or cream cheese and Jell-O desserts. The source of the ingredients matters because it's what carries the nutrients. So, it's important to opt for the organic and grass-fed instead of the conventional versions. It's also important to include leafy greens and other nutrient-dense vegetables as part of a well-balanced keto lifestyle. One note on this: Roberto, the man I worked with and one of my inspirations for this book (see the case study on page 6), was not eating organic or clean meats because they didn't fit into his budget, and he *still* saw amazing results. It just shows how powerful removing carbs and sugar can be even if you do not have access to the best-quality protein and fats. However, I do not recommend this.

Remember, you will be getting way more bang for your buck when choosing the high-quality products. When you eat factory-farmed meat, you're consuming everything that animal was exposed to throughout his or her life. In other words, you are eating the hormones, antibiotics, and inflammatory fats from those animals. Stay away from packaged convenience "keto"-labeled foods with low-carb sweeteners such as sucralose and Splenda. Most people who eat this unhealthy way of keto are not focusing on all the healthy veggies, go way too heavy on conventional dairy and meats, and do not eat enough vegetables.

# FOLLOWING A KETO DIET

## FOODS TO EAT

| | |
|---|---|
| **PROTEINS** | Grass-fed or pasture-raised beef, pork and poultry, organ meats, wild game, eggs, wild-caught fatty fish and seafood |
| **DAIRY** | All full-fat, organic, grass-fed milk, butter and cream, yogurt, and cheese |
| **HEALTHY FATS** | Avocados and avocado oil; nuts and seeds; nut butters; ghee; animal fats such as tallow, lard, and duck fat; coconut cream and oil; olives and olive oil |
| **NONSTARCHY VEGGIES** | Leafy greens, cucumbers, green beans, broccoli, asparagus, mushrooms, peppers, tomatoes, artichokes, cauliflower, brussels sprouts, cabbage, radishes, snap peas, onions, garlic |
| **CONDIMENTS** | Mayonnaise, mustards, vinegars, coconut aminos, hot sauce (although make sure they have no added sweeteners), salt, pickled and fermented veggies |

## FOODS TO AVOID

| | |
|---|---|
| **GRAINS** | Wheat, cereal, gluten, oats, couscous |
| **BEANS AND LEGUMES** | Chickpeas, peanuts, pinto beans, white and black beans |
| **UNHEALTHY OR PROCESSED OILS** | Vegetable oils; canola, corn, peanut, and soybean oils |
| **FRUIT** | All fruit except berries |
| **ALL SUGAR** | Granulated and brown sugar, artificial sweeteners, high-fructose corn syrup, honey, agave syrup, maple syrup |
| **STARCHY VEGGIES** | Tubers and corn (any corn by-product) |

## KETO IS NOT NEW

With the growing number of books, articles, and TV shows available today that celebrate the power of good fats, this information is finally becoming more accessible to the masses. There is a profound amount of research that shows a high-fat or ketogenic diet can reduce inflammation and, hence, disease, and the medical community is taking heed. Doctors have been using ketosis (high-fat, carb-restricted diets) as a treatment for epilepsy since the 1920s. Neurological conditions such as Alzheimer's and Parkinson's have been successfully treated with a high-fat diet, as have other serious illnesses such as cancer, metabolic syndrome, digestive disorders, migraines, and various psychological issues. Diseases such as diabetes, nonalcoholic fatty liver disease (NAFLD), obesity, autism, Alzheimer's, cancer, and heart disease all have one thing in common: they are rooted in insulin and leptin resistance, which both produce inflammatory and cellular damage. A diet high in fat and low in carbohydrates works to reduce inflammation in the body and mitigates cellular damage as a result.

Studies show that controlled insulin levels can optimize the metabolism and slow down the aging process. Glucose, insulin, and triglyceride levels tend to rise with age. Maintaining a high-sugar, high-carb diet prevents the body from sending the signal to burn fat because it can't access the fat stores. In contrast, a high-fat diet allows your body to access these stored fats and burn them more efficiently instead of using sugar (glucose).

## INFLAMMATION AND DISEASE

Inflammation is the body's innate response to stressors such as lack of sleep, acidic and highly processed foods, environmental toxins, disease, injury, and even the common cold. For example, when you bump an elbow and the area becomes swollen and bruised, that's the body's way of sending an inflammatory response signal. Symptoms of inflammation include swelling and bruising, redness, and pain. Very simply put, the body sends blood cells and fluid to the injured area to begin the healing process.

This acute example of bumping an elbow is important to understand, because it demonstrates how the body protects and heals itself. The blood flow, redness, swelling, and pain are all mechanisms that allow the body to heal. Unfortunately, internal inflammation is not always as obvious as a swollen elbow, nor is it a sign of healing but instead an indication of chronic issues. In many cases, it takes place internally, harmfully affecting our bodies without our knowing.

Inflammation can also occur on a cellular level. Our bodies are made up of trillions of cells. These cells, just like a bruised elbow, can become inflamed through environment, diet, lifestyle, or injury. When acute inflammation caused by environment, diet, or lifestyle occurs and those factors do not change, the inflammation becomes a constant state, as opposed to a temporary condition for healing. Chronic inflammation is the underlying cause of most disease.

Whether or not we realize it, we're all walking around with some form of inflammation in our bodies always. I'm here to help you apply inflammatory-reducing methods to your daily life. Not only will you look and feel younger, but you'll significantly lower your risk of developing chronic diseases. Plus, eating the right foods will help you manage any existing chronic diseases.

The best way to reduce inflammation is by changing your diet. The first step is to eliminate the primary sources of inflammation: sugars, food additives, preservatives, processed foods, and toxins. Unfortunately, conventional methods are killing our food on the molecular level, leaving no nutritional value and shocking our bodies, which creates an inflammatory response. These empty calories are labeled as food although they lack all the characteristics of real nourishment, such as fiber, vitamins, minerals, prebiotics, and probiotics. By focusing on nutrient-dense foods, ones high in healthy fats and clean proteins, along with consuming tons of organic vegetables, you will create an anti-inflammatory environment in the body.

Working with a wide range of clients suffering from inflammatory diseases over the last decade, I have learned that integrating a combination of balancing hormones, hacking sleep, eating clean and nutrient-dense food, hydrating, supporting the adrenal system, reducing stress, meditating, limiting toxic load, and exercising always yields great results.

Through the keto method that I outline, you will optimize your health, increase longevity, and lose weight. I know that some of you picked up this book with the primary focus of losing weight. I encourage you to chill on that point. I have found that people who obsess about weight loss struggle the most to actually lose weight. Many diets don't have a long-term focus toward sustainable health, and that is why keto is more of a lifestyle shift. My advice is to concentrate on how much better you feel daily, which will do a better job of keeping you motivated than hopping on the scale each morning. Before you know it, any extra weight you have been carrying around will be gone, and your overall health will be greatly improved.

## INTERMITTENT FASTING

Fasting is something we do every night. It's called sleep, hence the word *break-fast* since we are breaking our nightly fast. Fasting is one of the most powerful health and longevity tools we have, and it costs us nothing. Fasting has also been a part of most major religions, including Islam, Christianity, and Buddhism. Cycling between periods of eating and fasting, besides having historical significance, can help you combat the modern-day problems of chronic inflammation

Intermittent fasting is the process where you do not eat for a certain amount of time, fasting for a set number of hours that day. There are many fasting protocols depending on whom you ask, but to me just starting to fast is a step in the right direction. Intermittent fasting is a powerful healing tool that creates amazing results by improving overall health, including autophagy (speeding up detoxification). As one of humanity's most powerful tools, it goes hand in hand with a high-fat diet. Fasting is the easiest health hack you can incorporate into your life given its proven benefits. Fasting has a high correlation with promoting human growth hormone, which allows us to burn fat, helps slow the aging process, and facilitates the building of muscles. Not only that, fasting is also one of the most effective ways to increase your longevity and metabolism.

Let me start out by highlighting these two common myths that I will be debunking:

1. Skipping breakfast ruins your metabolism, causing your body to hang on to fat.

2. You must eat every couple of hours to balance your blood sugar.

### MY APPROACH

I have practiced intermittent fasting for just over four years now, and it is one of the biggest factors that has contributed to me simplifying my day, feeling my best, and really thriving (without hunger pangs and mood swings). As you know, I love to cook and, more important, eat, but having one less meal to plan saves me a lot of time and headspace in the day.

Implementing fasting into my client protocols has yielded incredible results across the board. From weight loss to increased productivity, it is truly beneficial for everyone. A quick note here: My female clients do much better when using a high-fat drink to substitute for their breakfast meal, which supports their hormonal balance, energy, and satiety.

For me, having a high-fat drink (see pages 48 to 49) with added MCT oil (similar to a "Bulletproof Coffee") allows me to extend my fasting window a few more hours. Usually, I go 16 to 18 hours without eating, although it does fluctuate. I do my best to listen to my body, and if I am hungry from a hard workout or stress, I will eat.

A high-fat drink for breakfast may be half addiction and half mind trick, but I'll take it. Occasionally, I'll just have plain black coffee or tea when I'm in a rush or in a fat-burning mode (ketosis), but most of the time I start my day with one of my high-fat drinks. The more keto adapted you are (not burning glucose anymore), the easier it is to fast. If you consume a high-fat drink with no protein or carbs, technically you're not breaking your fast. Some argue that because fats are calories, you are in fact breaking the fast, so if you want to be strict, stick to black coffee, tea, bone broth, or water (or switch off between the two options). However you choose to approach intermittent fasting, you will still gain massive, long-term benefits.

### EXAMPLE OF MY DAILY SCHEDULE

**6:30 A.M.** Wake up. Meditate. Drink one large glass of water with Himalayan salt, apple cider vinegar, and lemon juice (see page 47).

**7:00 A.M.** Have a high-fat drink (see pages 48 to 49).

**8:00 A.M.** Work out. Exercise while fasting has great results, especially high-intensity interval training (HIIT).

**12:00PM - 2:00 P.M.** Eat lunch. This is where the fast is broken, at sixteen to eighteen hours.

**7:00 P.M.** Eat dinner and close my eating window around 8:00 p.m. (giving me five to six hours of time-restricted eating).

**9:30 P.M.** Sleep.

Time-restricted eating is a form of intermittent fasting where you eat only during a certain set of hours. The one I do most often is a six- to eight-hour window of eating and then fasting for sixteen hours or more. This practice is also known as "sixteen to eight" (that's still a lot of eating—trust me, you can do it!). Among other optimal benefits, shortening your eating window (the time period from your first meal to your last) has shown to be very effective for longevity. You'll reap optimal benefits as you shorten your eating window. Eating lunch at 12:00 p.m., dinner at 7:00 p.m., and ending at 8:00 p.m. is the most realistic method I have found but you can adjust to what best fits your schedule. You can have one of my high-fat morning drinks or bone broth as your breakfast, which makes the fasting more comfortable and easier. Fasting gives your body a break from digestion, a process that takes tons of work and energy that can be redirected to other pathways.

## HOW DO YOU START FASTING?

There are many ways to start, but I have found that skipping breakfast is easiest for my clients. Skipping breakfast puts sixteen to eighteen hours in between dinner and the next meal (lunch), most of which is spent sleeping. I suggest doing this four to five times a week to start.

Once your body adjusts, you'll forget about those cravings. This is something that I didn't believe when I read all the research. How could ketogenic eating paired with fasting curb cravings and not make you so hangry? I swear to you that I can have a healthy lunch and that's it—no 3:00 p.m. slump coupled with a mad dash to get a sweet pick-me-up. Usually I would need a chocolate or anything I could get my hands on that was sugary. Now it doesn't even cross my mind! My favorite cookie can be staring me in the eye, and I can just walk away completely satisfied. That said, I am human, and I do indulge on the weekends— pizza, cocktails, and some vino.

## BREAKING YOUR FAST

I do not think there is a one-size-fits-all solution for what to eat after your fast. The most important thing about breaking your fast is to do it with proper fuel. Personally, I try to listen to how hungry I am. If I've worked out, I'll usually have a lunch containing lots of veggies, fats, and meats or seafood. Other times, I'll just do a big mason jar of bone broth, spices, and greens and then I'll have a handful of nuts a couple hours later, which satisfies me.

Intermittent fasting has been one of the most effective tools across the board for all of my clients. Whether they're facing serious disease or illness, looking to lose weight, or simply wanting to optimize their health, the biohack of intermittent fasting has offered them great success. Personally, it has been life changing in my own health journey, and if you've tried it, you know. If you haven't yet, what are you waiting for?

## BENEFITS OF FASTING

When you don't eat for a while, some GOOD things start to happen in your body. Here's a list of the many benefits of fasting.

- Reduces insulin and leptin sensitivity

- Lowers blood sugar levels

- Increases metabolism

- Elevates your growth hormone (helping you put on lean muscle and burn stored fat)

- Reduces belly fat and increases weight loss (by improving fat burning)

- Reduces inflammation and free radical damage

- Improves blood pressure, total and LDL cholesterol, and blood triglycerides

- Increases waste removal from cells (autophagy)

- Increases cognitive function and mental clarity and reduces brain fog

- Reduces hunger by increasing ghrelin, the hormone that stops us from overeating

- Helps prevent neurodegenerative diseases such as Alzheimer's, dementia, and Parkinson's

- Improves detoxification

- Improves gut health

- Stimulates mitochondria production (cellular repair, optimizing energy)

- Improves biomarkers across the board (meaning fasting has been shown to improve biomarkers such as glucose, Creative protein or CRP, insulin, and cholesterol)

- Shifts metabolism from using glucose energy to burning ketones (making you fat adapted—an efficient fat burner)

## SUPPLEMENTS AND RECOMMENDATIONS

Unfortunately, we are lacking some essential nutrients and vitamins thanks to commercial food systems, factory farms, conventional produce, and environmental toxins. So we need to supplement our diet. But beware, the supplement industry is not regulated, meaning they could be selling you a form you cannot absorb, additives, colors, fillers, allergens, GMOs, toxic material, and many other ingredients.

Taking just a few good-quality supplements daily can step up your health game and allow you to feel your best. I recommend speaking with your functional medicine doctor or nutritionist to create a personalized supplement protocol for you.

B COMPLEX: This is one group that people are very deficient in. It is essential for DNA repair, homocysteine level balance, and energy in the body. I recommend a sublingual 250 mg to 1 g daily.

CANNABIDIOL (CBD): Think of CBD as a multivitamin that reduces inflammation in our bodies. With the increasing popularity of CBD, the market is becoming more saturated with options, but not all are created equal. LEEF Organics stands apart from the rest of the current CBD brands and is known for its high-quality growing and extraction processes that use the whole flower, which helps with absorption and bioavailability. Through extensive research, personal trial, and hundreds of client testimonials, I can highly recommend LEEF Organics. Use 2 drops under your tongue twice a day.

FISH OIL (OMEGAS & KRILL OIL): These essential fats help to reduce inflammation. The main things to look for when choosing a fish oil is absorption, purity (no heavy metals from large, farm-raised fish), freshness, sustainability (choose only wild), and bioavailability. I suggest 500 mg a day unless you have a chronic disease, in which case take 1 to 2 g a day. Brands I like are Jarrow and Vital Choice. Always store in the fridge.

MAGNESIUM: Most of us are deficient in this essential micronutrient, and it is responsible for more than three hundred metabolic processes in the body. Magnesium comes in many different forms. Glycenite is great for sleep, citrate helps to calm, sulfate and malate work for muscle soreness, and oxide works for constipation. I take 200 to 800 mg in the day plus Natural Vitality Calm Powder at night and I sleep better and have better elimination, muscle recovery, and less anxiety. I also recommend taking Epsom salt (1 to 2 cups) baths at night, in which you absorb the magnesium through your skin.

ADAPTOGENS: Simply put, they help us to better handle things such as stress. But that's not all—not even close. They also support a resilient immune system, help with cognitive function, promote blood sugar balance, offer anti-inflammatory properties, offer antiaging properties, improve respiratory function, improve sleep, increase energy levels, and balance hormones. I suggest Root and Bones, a vibrant holistic herb company, or Host Defense. I put ¼ teaspoon of either reishi, he shou wu, chaga, lion's mane, cordyceps, pine pollen, or rhodiola in my high-fat drink (see pages 48 to 49) every morning, and I have not been sick in years.

**PROBIOTICS:** In addition to eating fermented foods, I highly suggest everyone should be on a probiotic supplement, but most on the shelf never make it to your gut. I suggest a shelf-stable one with 10 billion to 20 billion CFUs. I recommend Microbiome Megaspore.

**VITAMIN C:** This is a powerful antioxidant that boosts our immune system, forms collagen, forms connective tissue, and helps with oxidative stress. You can get vitamin C through food, but I recommend taking minimum 500 mg to 2 g ascorbic acid crystal or liposomal when you are feeling like your immune system needs a boost, when you are traveling, and so forth. You know you've taken too much when you have loose stools.

**VITAMIN D₃:** Vitamin D is known as the "sunshine vitamin" and is one of the most important supplements. Most people are low or deficient in vitamin D, which contributes to lower mood, low energy, inflammation, weakened immunity, and higher risk for certain types of cancer. Ideally, you want your vitamin D level on your lab test to be between 60 and 80. I see way too many of my clients' vitamin D levels below 40 when tested. Ask your doctor to test your levels. If you are low, supplementing with vitamin D will help to bring your levels back up. You can supplement with between 2,000 to 10,000 IU per day (in pill or liquid form) and then retest three months later to see where your levels are.

## COLLAGEN

Want to have longer hair and nails, fewer wrinkles, and tighter skin? Well, it is time to add collagen to your life! Collagen is the primary building block of skin, hair, nails, bones, tendons, joints, and cartilage. I like to tell people to think about it as the glue that holds the body together. The body's natural production of collagen starts to slow down as we age, which is the reason for wrinkles, thin skin, brittle hair, and weaker cartilage in your joints. Unfortunately, when convenience foods were introduced, we all stopped consuming the traditional foods that contained these crucial nutrients. In nature, collagen is found exclusively in animal tissue, especially bones and connective tissue. When purchasing, always choose a company that is sourced from pasture-raised and grass-fed animals. Make sure it is in a glass or BPA-free container. Add 1 to 2 tablespoons daily to your morning drink (see pages 48 to 49). I suggest using with a good vitamin C supplement to best optimize your absorption.

### OTHER PLACES TO FIND COLLAGEN

- **BONE BROTH:** Of course, bone broth (see page 120) has it but not as much as we need. I recommend adding collagen powder to your bone broth and soups.

- **COLLAGEN POWDER:** This type is broken down into individual peptide chains that are easier to digest for most people. It is easy to add to your routine because it is tasteless and odorless. It also gives your food a thicker consistency.

- **GELATIN:** This is what you typically see when you take out your cooled bone broth when it becomes gelatinous. This form is more jellylike, hence it is great for making gummies, marshmallow, and desserts. (See Collagen Panna Cotta, page 197.)

## MORE WAYS TO BOOST YOUR IMMUNE SYSTEM ALL YEAR-ROUND SO YOU NEVER GET SICK

**ADAPTOGENS:** These plant-based remedies help the body adapt to stressors. They have been used in ancient traditions around the world to bring the body back into balance. Specifically, adaptogens such as reishi, ashwaganda, and astragalus help to boost the immune system.

**COLLOIDAL SILVER (FOR NOSE, EARS, AND THROAT):** Silver can block bacteria cells and naturally holds on to oxygen molecules, making it antibacterial and antimicrobial.

**ELDERBERRY SYRUP:** This derivative of elderberries is high in antioxidants and vitamin C, and helps with respiratory infections. It also shortens the duration of cold and flu symptoms.

**EPSOM SALTS AND ESSENTIAL OIL BATHS:** Epsom salts are high in magnesium, which helps the body relax and detoxify. Essential oils help with immune-system support. Frankincense, clove, oregano, and rosemary are all great for boosting the immune system and strengthening the body.

**OIL OF OREGANO:** This antiviral, antimicrobial remedy can destroy bacteria, viruses, and candida.

## COOKING OILS

Understanding cooking oils, cooking temperatures, smoke points, and benefits are all essential to healthy living. Remember that fat is flavor, but it needs to be treated and used correctly to reap all the benefits.

### MISUSING OILS

I talk a lot about oils with my clients—heating, cooking, types, fat properties, smoke points, and oxidation. As you can see throughout the book, olive oil is only used when controlling a temperature, on top of raw veggies, or for salad dressings. Heating olive oil can destroy its healthy properties. When an oil is heated beyond its smoke point, meaning where it will actually smoke and become oxidized, it creates free radicals (the bad guys), which in turn create inflammation. Of course, occasionally misusing oils for flavor profiles will not kill you, but why not get the best out of the oils?

When you hear an oil is or can become unstable, it means the oil is vulnerable to oxidation. The fat goes rancid, therefore creating free radicals that cause oxidative damage to our cells. These types of unstable vegetable fats (polyunsaturated, trans fats) become rancid just by exposure to light through the bottle. Heat as well as air and pressure oxidize these types of fat.

The industrial oils from canola oil to Crisco are all treated chemically with things such as glyphosate and then processed again to have a long shelf life so that they never go bad. Most of the vegetables and seeds used to make these oils (canola, safflower, and grapeseed) were grown for industrial use, meaning they were treated chemically, which is problematic when added to products that undergo light, air, and pressure. Stay far away from these oils.

All oils should be stored in a cool, dark area, away from heat and light. When high-quality oil is exposed to light and heat, it becomes oxidized (oxidation is bad; think wrinkles or an avocado turning brown). If you live in a warm climate, you should refrigerate your oils so they do not turn rancid. A good indication that your oils should be refrigerated is if your coconut oil is liquid; it should not be. Also, dark containers are best if you can find them. After you've opened the oil, try to use it within one month. (This is one reason why large or big bulk bottles are not a good idea.)

## THE BEST OILS

MCT OIL: Medium-chain triglyceride (MCT) oil is a powerful biohack to have in your pantry for both the body and brain. MCTs are a special type of saturated fat that our bodies can turn into energy very quickly. MCT is extracted from coconut oil (stay away from palm oil) and comes in four strains of carbon: $C_6$, $C_8$, $C_{10}$, and $C_{12}$. Make sure you choose MCT oil from a good source, and carefully read the label. If it makes you feel sick or you have to run to the bathroom, it's probably not the best for you.

Brain Octane and XCT Oil by Bulletproof are different from most MCT oils. Bulletproof is the most effective source of MCT on the market. It raises ketones in the body more quickly than other MCTs because of how it is made. They are *not* generic MCT oils, which is about 1.6 times stronger than coconut oil (which is now being sold all over). You would need about 22 tablespoons of coconut oil to get the same benefits as Brain Octane.

By using a high-quality MCT oil, you will increase your fat burning and mental clarity, curb hunger and sugar cravings, and increase your energy. Who wouldn't want to try it? It makes me think clearer and be more productive, gives me energy, helps absorb other nutrients by making them more bioavailable, helps produce ketones, makes me feel full longer, and lessens cravings.

Here are the facts:

- Almost all companies (except Bulletproof) use solvents or bleach to clean and deodorize their MCT oil, which can leave trace chemicals in the final product.

- It is best to stay away from solvents, palm oils, and emulsifiers.

- You should choose MCT from a sustainable coconut oil source.

MCT oil can be used in my high-fat drinks on pages 48 to 49 and for salad dressings, sauces, roasted veggies, and marinating.

AVOCADO OIL: This oil is high in monounsaturated fat; vitamins A, D, E, and $K_2$; and oleic acid. It helps us absorb the nutrients of the food it coats when used for sautéing, frying, and searing. It has a high smoke point of 520°F. Choose organic, unrefined, and cold-pressed avocado oil.

COCONUT OIL: Solid at room temperature, coconut oil is great for Asian cooking, roasting veggies, and as a nondairy baking alternative to replace butter. The smoke point is 350°F. I also love coconut oil as a makeup remover, moisturizer for dry skin, and a hair mask.

**DUCK AND CHICKEN FAT:** These fats are semisolid at room temperature and are great for frying at higher temperatures.

**OLIVE OIL:** A high-quality olive oil is so pure that it should be left unaltered; in other words it should not be heated unless at a controlled temperature. Use it for low-heat cooking and for finishing dishes (a drizzle on top of cooked steak or fish) to reap all the benefits. It goes without saying that it's great for salad dressings as well.

This tasty liquid contains about 75 percent oleic acid—a stable monounsaturated fat—and antioxidants, which can help in stabilizing blood sugar levels and reducing inflammation throughout the body. Low-quality olive oil will burn because it has less acid, has been cut with vegetable oils, and may have particulate matter from not being separated properly. If possible, stay away from conventional grocery stores when purchasing your oil. Buy from a producer or a certified distributor, and look for the International Olive Oil Council certification. I like to stick with small farms when purchasing olive oil.

**GRASS-FED BUTTER:** Grass-fed butter is back and for a good (and delicious) reason. It's rich in beta-carotene; vitamins A, D, E, and K; omega-3s; and conjugated linoleic acid (CLA), which helps protect us from inflammatory disease, boosts immunity, and has strong anticancer properties. It also contains butyrate, which helps bacteria in our gut, boosts energy, and also boosts our metabolism. Yes, butter is amazing for us! It has a smoke point of 350°F. (Note that grain-fed butter does not contain these amazing benefits.)

**GRASS-FED GHEE:** With a high smoke point of 485°F, ghee is great for sautéing and searing meat, plus is a great butter substitute for my dairy-free amigos. I use both this and grass-fed butter daily depending on what I am cooking or the flavors I want.

**PASTURE-RAISED LARD:** Lard is stable and is a preferred fat for cooking at higher temperatures.

## SUPERFOODS

You do not need a huge amount of these guys because they are naturally concentrated and nutritionally dense powerhouses containing high amounts of nutrients, including antioxidants, fiber, phytonutrients, vitamins, and minerals. Quality ingredients are essential for flavor and health. As Julia Child once said, "You don't have to cook fancy or complicated masterpieces—just good food from fresh ingredients."

**ALOE VERA:** Aloe grows easily in most subtropical parts of Mexico and is a natural anti-inflammatory. I promise, it's not just for sunburn. It is well known for healing skin issues, but what about eating it in a smoothie or juicing it raw as a drink? The whole leaf (skin on) helps with digestion and constipation. The inner aloe flesh soothes the gut, improves immunity, and reduces inflammation. So, when you drink it, thank that powerful plant you see, well, everywhere.

**APPLE CIDER VINEGAR WITH THE MOTHER:** This is a staple in my kitchen because it lowers cholesterol and blood sugar, and it contributes to weight loss. This living vinegar offers many nutritional benefits, including aiding in digestion, reducing inflammation, and relieving digestion upset. Organic, unpasteurized apple cider vinegar has sediment in the bottom of the bottle, known as the mother, and that's where all the benefits lie. Make sure you purchase vinegar with the mother.

**AVOCADOS:** Avocados, my favorite healthy fat and also one of the world's most nutrient-dense foods, contain more potassium than a banana. Filled with oleic acid, lutein, folate, vitamin E, and monounsaturated fats, avocados help with brain and cognitive function. They're also great for hormone balance and blood sugar regulation. You can peel and freeze them for smoothies, or you can make Probiotic Guacamole (page 91) or my Cacao Avocado Mousse (page 200).

**BEE POLLEN:** Pollen is considered one of nature's most complete nourishing foods as it contains nearly all nutrients required by humans. Rich in proteins; amino acids; vitamins, including B-complex; and folic acid, bee pollen is great for strengthening immunity and combating seasonal allergies. Put 1 teaspoon in your smoothies or add it to your breakfast yogurt.

**BLUE-GREEN ALGAE, CHLORELLA, AND SPIRULINA:** These are organisms that are all in the same family. They are high in protein, minerals, and carotenoids. The Aztecs in Mexico ate them as a staple food dried on tortillas.

**CACAO:** Cacao is filled with antioxidants that boost your immune system, plus it tastes amazing. When mixed into recipes, its rich flavor is delicious and dessert-like, which helps you resist those sugar cravings while still satisfying your sweet tooth.

Cacao is different from cocoa, but they start from the same place. Cacao powder has antioxidants and more health benefits because it is raw and processed at low temperatures. Cocoa has been roasted at high temperatures and then mixed with fillers, like dairy products and sugar. Cocoa powder is used in conventional baking and as a hot chocolate mix. Cocoa has been stripped of any health benefits through processing.

**CACAO NIBS:** The nibs are peeled and crumbled cacao beans, rich in magnesium, iron, and antioxidants. They are not sweet but are a perfect crunch to add to your desserts or trail mix, or to just snack on alone.

**CAYENNE PEPPER:** This helps speed up warming and metabolism in the body.

**CEYLON CINNAMON:** This is an antioxidant that helps balance blood sugar, especially after coming off of a fast or when practicing intermittent fasting.

**CHAYOTE:** You may have seen this green pear-shaped vegetable at the store. It is crunchy like a potato but has a clean flavor similar to zucchini or cucumber. It is used in Mexico in soups, with eggs, or just roasted alone. It is high in fiber and rich in folate.

**CHIA SEEDS:** Chia seeds are loaded with antioxidants, protein, and minerals, plus soluble and insoluble fiber to help keep your digestion moving in the right direction. Chia seeds also contain a high content of omega fatty acids that increase healthy brain function and have proven to be good for your heart. Use 1 tablespoon a day in your smoothies, in water with lemon (see page 47), or to thicken desserts!

**CHILES:** See "Understanding Chiles" on page 59.

**CILANTRO:** Cilantro is one of the oldest herbs in history. It is both an herb and a spice because of the seeds from the plant called coriander (if you have any English or Aussie friends, you know this is what they call cilantro). Cilantro is a binder and a detoxifier, ridding you of heavy metals. It is proven to have antifungal, antiseptic, and antibacterial properties. Cilantro is packed with vitamins A, E, and K and many essential minerals. If you let your cilantro go to seed (make a flower), it becomes a delicious and beautiful garnish to any dish, which I learned from the food stylist at my photo shoot.

**COCONUT PRODUCTS:** The heart-healthy oil in coconut products are filled with antioxidants that can help your body fight viruses and the bacteria that can cause illness. It can also boost thyroid function and blood-sugar control as well as aid with digestion, reduce cholesterol, and keep weight balanced. Coconut contains fatty acids that help to fight body fat by converting it into energy that boosts metabolism. I use coconut oil when I cook anything on high heat.

- Coconut milk, water, and flesh oil can be used for anything from beauty products to foods.
- The products support immune-system health because they are antiviral, antibacterial, antifungal, and antiparasitic.
- They can produce MCT, which is a by-product of coconut oil.
- Its high-fiber, low-carb content increases your metabolism.
- Coconut flour is gluten- and grain-free and great for baking.

**EDIBLE FLOWERS:** The following edible flowers add color and flavor for both salads and desserts: chive flower, nasturtium, garlic flower, and lavender. Top tacos or salads for a beautiful finishing touch. Just like everything else, it's important to source organic or pesticide-free flowers for eating

**EGGS:** Egg yolks contain brain-boosting nutrients and are a great source of protein and fat. They are very versatile and are best eaten on the runny side. Always choose pasture-raised.

**EPAZOTE:** An herb traditionally used in Mexico for cooking and medicine, epazote is closely related to oregano, with hints of mint and citrus. It has dark green, jagged leaves and is found mostly dried, unless you get it fresh at a Mexican specialty store or farmers' market (you can freeze it for later, too). Use in beans, soups, and meat dishes.

**ESCABECHE:** This is a Spanish word describing a pickling method. When vegetables are fermented or pickled, good bacteria is formed, which feeds our immune system and gut. See more on page 144.

**GARLIC:** I have met only one person who does not like garlic. I have had clients who needed to remove it for a bit, but not by choice. It is always in my kitchen and not only tastes amazing but is also antibacterial and anti-inflammatory, packed with vitamins, great for the immune system (chew it up), serves as a mosquito repellent, and even helps with ear infections!

**HIMALAYAN SALT:** It is high in minerals and is great for adrenal health (balancing cortisol) if you add a dash to your water first thing in the morning (see page 47).

**LARD:** Lard has been enjoyed for thousands of years and varies significantly based on the approach to raising and feeding the hogs. The Weston A. Price Foundation discovered that lard from pasture-raised pigs contained 10,000 IU of vitamin D per 1 tablespoon—that's *hundreds of times* the amount in the USDA food database (which is based on conventionally raised hogs). Lard is packed with omega-3s, is heat stable and therefore great for high-heat cooking, and has a neutral flavor.

**MACA:** Maca is a phytochemical classified as an adaptogen (helping balance) that helps with boosting energy, balancing hormones, and increasing libido and fertility in men and women. It is rich in mood-boosting B vitamins and brain-boosting compounds. Its earthy, caramel taste is great in my high-fat coffee (see page 48), smoothies, or desserts.

**MEXICAN OREGANO:** This is a cousin of lemon verbena and is native to Mexico. It's pungent like Mediterranean oregano, and Mexican oregano has notes of mild licorice and citrus.

**MORINGA:** This has been nicknamed "miracle tree" for a good reason. All parts of the moringa plant are beneficial, but the most powerful parts are the seeds and leaves. It's antimicrobial, anti-inflammatory, and rich in antioxidants. Rich in iron, potassium, vitamin C, and vitamin A, moringa may be the most nutrient-rich plant per gram than any other. It is helpful in lowering blood sugars (I recommend it often to my patients because it is affordable and does a really good job), losing weight, and reducing overall inflammation. Add it your water, teas, matcha, soups, desserts, and smoothies.

**NUTRITIONAL YEAST:** A natural source of B vitamins, nutritional yeast is great for people who do not eat red meat. It has a natural cheesy and nutty flavor and is a great way to make a dairy-free cheese, such as my Vegan Cashew Spread (page 72).

**PEPITAS:** This is a term for pumpkin seeds. Pepitas are packed with minerals such as zinc, phosphorus, and magnesium and also contain protein and healthy fats.

**SEAWEEDS (KELP, DULSE, KOMBU):** Seaweeds are nutritionally dense plants as they have access to all the nutrients in the ocean. They can contain up to ten times more calcium than milk and eight times as much as beef. The chemical composition of seaweeds is so close to human blood plasma that perhaps their greatest benefit is regulating and purifying our blood system.

**TURMERIC:** This spice contains antioxidants and antiseptic and anti-inflammatory components. It is an Indian spice that gives a distinctive taste and contains a compound called curcumin (that turns everything it touches, including your skin, bright yellow). This powerful superstar helps with everything from headaches, circulation and blood clotting to pain, inflammation, and a lot more. Spice up your recipes by adding 1 teaspoon turmeric powder or fresh turmeric root. But before you sprinkle it on everything you eat, know that, first off, it is fat soluble, meaning it needs a fat such as avocado oil or coconut oil. Second, it needs black pepper (piperine), which improves the bioavailability by 2,000 percent. The third element is heat. It needs to be heated (a high-powered blender counts).

## HOW TO USE SALT

Not all salt is created equal, but salt is essential in your diet. Most people are either using the wrong ones or are scared of it. The studies on how salt is detrimental to your health are done with horrific table salt. That is the salt to stay away from. Some are saltier than others with different textures and densities, mineral, and sodium content. If a recipe calls for Himalayan and you use kosher, the dish might not come out as salty as it should. I recommend choosing and using unrefined sources of salt, because that way, you receive the minerals and micronutrient properties the salt naturally contains. I personally use Himalayan, Maldon, Jacobsen, and kosher salt in my kitchen. When on a keto diet, minerals are essential, so choose a high-quality salt and don't be scared to salt your food; your body needs it.

- **HIMALAYAN:** This type of salt helps balance the body's pH and contains about eighty-four minerals along with trace elements such as magnesium, potassium, iron, and calcium. It has a saltier flavor than other salts and is the most beneficial salt.

- **KOSHER SALT:** This is a favorite among chefs. It has no added iodine or caking agents, and it dissolves instantly and evenly when cooking.

- **MALDON SALT:** This flaky salt works well for finishing meat or salads. It's English, kosher approved, and small batched.

- **SEA SALT (CELTIC):** Made from evaporated ocean water, sea salt contains more minerals than table salt. Its source matters because of this evaporation process. Things such as plastics and other contaminants have been found in certain sea salts.

- **IODIZED SALT (TABLE SALT):** It's cheap and not rich in minerals like the rest of the options mentioned above. It's heavily processed and is also known as refined salt, meaning its impurities and trace minerals are taken out and then it is bleached, leaving just sodium (and way more than other salts). Iodine and caking agents are added.

# KETO REFRIGERATOR AND FREEZER STAPLES

**APPLE CIDER VINEGAR:** Take a shot before meals, or add it to your salad dressing. It helps with skin issues, digestion, acid reflux, and is a must when you are sick.

**BERRIES:** Rich in antioxidants, berries are the answer for your sweet tooth. These sweet treats are one of my favorite snacks or summertime treats, in moderation.

**BONE BROTH:** This nutritional powerhouse is essential for healing inflammation and gut issues. It can be used in stir-fry, to cook your rice, or to sip. Told you food can be medicine.

**CAULIFLOWER RICE:** Now that Trader Joe's and Costco carry frozen riced cauliflower, I always have it on hand. Try it in meatballs, see Sopa de Albondigas (page 125).

**EXTRA-DARK CHOCOLATE:** I can think of one reason, ahem, time of the month, when high-percent cacao should always be on hand. Another great one to keep in your freezer. Choose 70 percent or higher.

**FERMENTED FOODS:** Sauerkraut, miso, kefir, kimchi . . . add on top of all things.

**FRESH HERBS:** Oh, the possibilities. Chop and mix your herbs with butter and then spoon them into ice cube trays and keep them in the freezer. Blend with garlic and olive oil to make a chimichurri. The list doesn't have to stop here.

**GRASS-FED BUTTER:** People are so scared of butter. Don't be. Our bodies and brain need it. Are we best friends yet? I always have this in my freezer.

**HIGH-QUALITY CHEESE:** I've won you over with this one, right? Use at least one but ideally all of the following: grass-fed, raw, pasture-raised, local, organic.

**LEAFY GREENS:** Keep fresh greens on hand and make it that much easier to incorporate them into your family's diet. I recommend making it a goal to try a new green once a week from the store, use tops of things such as radishes (see page 142) and carrots for pesto.

**NUT BUTTER:** The perfect snack garnish. Spread on your favorite veggies and fruits.

**NUTS:** Always buy raw. I love to keep them in the freezer to prevent the fat from oxidizing and turning rancid.

**OLIVES:** High in good fats, olives are great additions to your snack menu. Guests will love them, too.

**PASTURE-RAISED EGGS:** I know there are many choices, but just choose pasture raised. This superfood, especially the yolk, has amino acids and essential brain food.

# KETO PANTRY STAPLES

**CANNED ANCHOVIES:** It's a superfood that gives complexity and immense flavor to your food, like in my Tijuana Caesar Dressing (page 111).

**CANNED WILD FISH:** Get European with wild sardines, mackerel, or salmon. Place atop salads or try with a crudité board (see page 80).

**CHIA SEEDS:** These tiny nutritional powerhouses are packed with fiber and protein and even help combat inflammation. Use in desserts and smoothies.

**CHIPOTLE PEPPERS IN ADOBO SAUCE:** The little can of chiles packs spicy and smoky depth of flavor in a creamy red sauce and is my secret weapon. I love it with my crema, compound butters, queso dip, salsa, or soup. You can freeze leftovers in ice cube trays, too!

**COCONUT OIL/MCT OIL:** A fat perfect for cooking using high-heat temperatures. Did you know it also contains antibacterial compounds that help boost fat burning? Where is the hug mechanism on this thing? These oils are shelf stable and do not need refrigeration.

**DRIED CHILES:** Now that you can cook Mexican food, you want all the chiles all the time, from mild to hot.

**DRIED MUSHROOMS:** Pour some water over them and you have mushrooms ready for a Mushroom Vegetarian Tostada with All the Toppings (page 224). Mushrooms have a delicious umami earthy flavor that is perfect to add to your favorite meal.

**DRIED SEAWEED:** One of the most nutrient-dense foods on the planet but so underused. Kombu, nori, arame, wakame, dulse, spirulina, chlorella, kelp, and algae are my choices. Keep a variety in your pantry to add to soups, salads, and broth and to get your boost of vitamins, minerals, and iodine!

**DRIED SPICES AND HERBS:** Use them as much as possible. They're superfoods, and they make your dishes delicious. Cinnamon is great for balancing blood sugar, and turmeric, well, you know all about those anti-inflammatory benefits by now.

**GARLIC:** Antiviral, tasty. Learn how to roast garlic and how to add them to your sauces. I'm here to help. How? See my Garlic Chile-Infused Everyday Oil (page 71).

**SAN MARZANO TOMATOES:** You already know I'm Mexican, but I have an incredible friend who is ninety-three years old and also happens to be my Italian grandpa. He introduced me to the best tomato, and now I'm introducing them to you.

# BREAKFAST

## DESAYUNO

The moment you tell your friends you skip "the most important meal of the day," they look at you like you are a crazy person. But contrary to popular belief, breakfast is not the most important meal of the day. Eating breakfast does not help you lose weight, speed up your metabolism, or balance your blood sugar. Especially not when most people's breakfasts consist of glyphosate-laden, carbohydrate-filled, and sugar-packed cereals, muffins, pancakes, and oatmeal. Of course, you can't lose weight or expect to have energy with that kind of toxic sugar blast!

Before I discovered intermittent fasting, I found that eating breakfast made me hungrier throughout the day. So, instead I consume a high-fat drink or even water rather than a meal, and this has been shown to help boost metabolism and train the body to burn fat instead of sugar.

NOTE The following drink variations are replacing your breakfast meal. If you need more calories, are pregnant or nursing, have a serious illness, or are an athlete, start on page 50.

## HIGH-FAT DRINKS

No matter if you are making your high-fat drink with coffee, matcha, black tea, green tea, or noncaffeinated tea, this is the best way to fuel your brain and body for a productive and energy-filled day. This routine should help to stabilize your blood sugar (although everyone has different eating habits and medical history).

Having a ritual in the morning sets up your day for success. After a good night's sleep, which is as important as nutrition, your body needs a couple of things right away. Remember that you have been fasting since dinner, so make sure you break it with the right nutrients for healing—in other words, fats.

I started this routine four years ago and have not looked back. I went from an insatiable hanger in the morning to feeling properly fueled without mood swings or cravings. I will occasionally eat breakfast on the weekends, but I never feel as energized and clearheaded as when I use this routine.

This chapter also contains high-fat, low-carb breakfast recipes that are perfect for the days you don't fast. They also don't have to be eaten only for breakfast. I love eating many of these recipes for a quick work lunch or dinner.

# ALKALIZING MORNING DRINK

**SERVES 2 • PREPARATION TIME 5 MINUTES**

Our bodies are about two-thirds water, so they need to be hydrated in order to carry out normal functions. Water helps our bodies detoxify, acts as a natural appetite suppressant, lubricates joints, and helps rev up our metabolism. Plus, without proper hydration, no matter how clean we eat or how much we exercise, we cannot absorb and assimilate our nutrients or even recover from our workouts!

Drink this as soon as you wake up. I put it in a big mason jar or glass pitcher and make it on the stronger side. I will add more water as I drink. Have at least 16 ounces of this water upon rising to ensure your day is as healthy as possible.

You can also skip the water and double or triple the other ingredients to make this more of a concentrate that you add to water each morning.

16 ounces cold or warm filtered water

2 to 4 tablespoons apple cider vinegar

2 tablespoons freshly squeezed lemon juice

½ teaspoon Ceylon cinnamon

Dash of cayenne pepper

Liquid stevia (optional; I like 5 drops per serving)

Dash of Himalayan salt

2 scoops chia seeds, inulin (prebiotic), or psyllium husk (optional)

½ teaspoon trace mineral drops (optional)

1. In a large glass cup or mason jar, stir together the water, vinegar, lemon juice, cinnamon, cayenne, liquid stevia (if using), and sea salt. If using chia seeds or trace mineral drops, stir them in as well. Drink first thing in the morning, or make a double batch and sip throughout the day.

# MEXICAN HIGH-FAT ("BULLETPROOF") COFFEE

2 tablespoons MCT oil

2 tablespoons Kerrygold grass-fed butter or ghee (use ghee if you have any dairy issues)

1 teaspoon Ceylon cinnamon

**ADDITIONS**

1 teaspoon Mexican cacao powder

1 teaspoon reishi, chaga, or lion's mane mushroom adaptogen powder

1 teaspoon maca powder

1 teaspoon pure vanilla extract, or 1 whole scraped vanilla bean

Liquid stevia (optional; I like 5 drops per serving)

16 ounces brewed organic coffee (can substitute decaf)

1 to 2 tablespoons pasture-raised collagen protein (optional)

**SERVES 2 • PREPARATION TIME 10 MINUTES**

So, most of you have heard about the butter in your coffee thing, right? To be honest, it has completely changed my life and the lives of so many of my clients, family, and friends. Plus, it tastes delish! Cinnamon has been shown to curb blood sugar by lowering insulin resistance, which is great for diabetics and for fasting. From my research, Ceylon cinnamon is the best because it's true cinnamon ground from the bark, unlike most other varieties that are made with fillers and cheaper alternatives. I also love Mexican cinnamon sticks, which you can grind in your coffee grinder!

1. Place the MCT oil in a blender with the butter, cinnamon, and any additions you are using. Add your freshly brewed coffee and blend on high speed for 10 to 15 seconds, until frothy and foamy.

2. If adding the collagen, stir it in at the very end. Do not blend because it will denature the proteins! Serve immediately.

## MY MORNING CAFÉ

Have you ever had a cup of coffee that made you feel horrible? Jitters, headache, nausea, upset stomach, or just not normal? Bad coffee can tank your energy and focus and make you crash badly (that's how drinking coffee with a fat can help). Well, there's a lot you might not know about what goes into that cup of joe. Not all coffee is created equal. Studies show that there are more chemicals in your coffee than in a pharmacy! Most coffee beans are rinsed with water and set in the sun to dry or crushed to ferment. During these types of processing, they can end up with mycotoxins, or mold. So, when choosing coffee, first choose organic and then shade grown, grown in Central America, small batched, and sustainably grown.

# HIGH-FAT MATCHA

**SERVES 2 • PREPARATION TIME 10 MINUTES**

Some people who cannot handle caffeine do better with matcha because it contains phytonutrients. One in particular, L-theanine (nature's Xanax), is an amino acid that helps our bodies process the caffeine differently, making it more of a sustained boost without the crash.

1.  In a blender, place the matcha tea powder, pour in the boiling water, and blend on low speed for about 10 seconds. Add the MCT oil, butter, and reishe and blend on low speed.

2.  In a small saucepan or a milk frother, bring the coconut milk to a simmer over medium heat. Add it to the blender along with the sweetener you desire. If you are adding the collagen, stir in at this point. Serve immediately.

2 to 3 teaspoons high-quality organic matcha tea powder (can subsitute decaf or any tea of choice such as chai, black, dandelion root)

1 cup boiling filtered water

2 tablespoons MCT oil

2 tablespoons Kerrygold grass-fed butter, ghee, coconut mana, or cacao butter

1 teaspoon reishe, chaga, or lion's mane mushroom adaptogen powder

1 cup coconut milk or any unsweetened nut milk

1 teaspoon liquid stevia or monk fruit sweetener (optional)

2 tablespoons pasture-raised collagen protein

# HIGH-FAT TEA

**SERVES 2 • PREPARATION TIME 10 MINUTES**

Bergamot tea helps with autophagy, insulin sensitivity, and blood sugar balance, which is especially important in the morning.

1.  In a kettle or medium saucepan, bring 2 cups of water to a boil. Pour the hot water into a heatproof glass or mason jar or just add the tea bags to the saucepan. Let the tea steep for at least 4 minutes, but ideally 10 minutes, and then remove and discard the tea bags.

2.  Pour the brewed tea into a blender. Add the MCT oil, butter, and cinnamon and blend on low speed for 10 to 15 seconds. Stir in the collagen (if using) and add the sweetener to taste. Serve immediately.

4 bergamot tea bags

2 tablespoons MCT oil

2 tablespoons Kerrygold grass-fed butter, ghee (use ghee if you have any dairy issues), coconut mana, or cacao butter

1 teaspoon Ceylon cinnamon

2 tablespoons pasture-raised collagen protein (optional)

1 teaspoon liquid stevia or monk fruit sweetener (optional)

# BAKED EGGS IN AVOCADO

6 avocados, halved

12 pasture-raised eggs

Kosher salt and freshly ground black pepper

¼ cup crumbled Cotija

¼ cup Charred Red Salsa with Serrano Chiles (page 64)

**SERVES 12 • PREPARATION TIME 25 MINUTES**

Packed with good fats and protein, this dish is a perfect way to start your day. Your heart and brain will thank you. Feel free to make one just for you. Plus, it's beautiful, easy for groups, and ideal for a Sunday brunch. The yolk is the healthiest part of the egg and is best consumed lightly cooked or raw, provided that it is pasture raised.

1. Preheat the oven to 450°F. Remove the stone from each avocado and scoop out a bit of the flesh (about 1 teaspoon) to create a hole big enough for the egg.

2. Arrange the avocados snugly in a small baking dish. Carefully break one egg into each avocado half. If you want, you can crack each egg into a ramekin first and then pour it into the avocado so you don't break the yolk. Season each avocado by sprinkling salt and pepper on top.

3. Bake the avocado-eggs for 15 to 20 minutes, until your desired consistency is reached. Remember, the runnier the yolk, the more nutrients your body will absorb, so keep it as runny as you can. Top each with Cotija cheese and serve with a side of Charred Red Salsa.

# RAMEKIN-BAKED EGGS

½ cup Salsa Bandera (page 62), plain chopped tomatoes, or a store-bought salsa

1 cup chopped leafy greens such as spinach, kale, mustard greens, or chard

4 pasture-raised eggs

Kosher salt and freshly ground black pepper

2 tablespoons goat cheese, Cotija, or shaved Parmesan

4 teaspoons chopped fresh herbs such as cilantro, parsley, dill, or chives

½ avocado, cubed

8 slices pasture-raised bacon, cooked and roughly chopped (optional)

**SERVES 4 • PREPARATION TIME 20 MINUTES**

This is a recipe that I enjoy for lunch, dinner, and breakfast. I like to make this on a weekend when friends are over, because it's easy and looks beautiful. Once you get the hang of it, you can sub in and out whatever vegetables you have in the fridge. If you have some chopped cooked bacon, throw it on top for an extra-crunchy treat. Or leave it off to keep this a vegetarian meal.

1. Preheat an oven to 400°F. Lightly coat four 8-ounce oven-safe ramekins with coconut oil or butter using a paper towel or spray.

2. Evenly spoon the salsa into the ramekins or dish and then layer the greens on top. I like to crack the eggs right into the ramekins, but you can also crack them into a measuring glass or a cup and then transfer so you do not break the yolk. Season with salt and pepper.

3. Bake for about 15 minutes, until the yolks are done to your liking. The eggs will continue to cook once they are out of the oven so be careful not to overcook. Sprinkle the cheese, fresh herbs, and avocado on top, and add the bacon before serving, if you so wish.

# HUEVOS RANCHEROS

**SERVES 4 • PREPARATION TIME 1 HOUR**

What better cure for a hangover than ranch eggs (literally from our friends' ranch) poached in a spicy red sauce on top of a crispy tortilla? Traditionally, they are served with beans and red rice (see pages 218 and 219) and sliced avocado. This dish is composed of simple inexpensive ingredients.

Note that the tortillas are traditionally corn, which are not keto. For a completely keto version, use Coconut Tortillas with Lard (page 209).

1. To make the sauce: Place the rehydrated chiles, tomatoes, onion, jalapeño, garlic, and salt in a small pot or saucepan and cover with cold filtered water. Simmer for 12 to 15 minutes, until the tomatoes are soft. Drain and reserve the boiling liquid.

2. Transfer the strained boiled mixture to a food processor or blender and blend on high until smooth. You can use the reserved boiling liquid if needed to add to the blender to make it more liquid. Strain the mixture into a medium skillet for a smooth texture. I like to spoon in some chunks, but that is up to you.

3. Crack the eggs on top of the sauce and simmer with the lid on until the desired consistency is reached. I like mine runny, so I poach mine for about 4 minutes, until the whites are no longer translucent.

4. If you are using tortillas, heat them in a medium cast-iron skillet in ¼ inch of avocado oil. Using tongs, flip them to heat and crisp and then place them on the plate. Top each tortilla with two eggs and the sauce.

5. Once plated, I like to top them off with Salsa Bandera, lime slices, sliced avocado, and, of course, some fresh ranchero cheese or feta and cilantro.

**SAUCE**

3 to 4 dried pasilla chiles, dry-roasted, stem and seeds removed, and rehydrated (see page 60)

4 whole tomatoes, halved (any kind will work)

1 cup coarsely chopped white onion

1 jalapeño, coarsely chopped

2 garlic cloves, minced

1 teaspoon kosher salt

8 pasture-raised eggs

8 corn or coconut tortillas (optional)

Avocado oil for the tortillas (optional)

Salsa Bandera (page 62) for topping

Lime slices for topping

2 avocados, sliced thin

Fresh ranchero cheese or feta for topping

Cilantro for garnish

# GOAT CHEESE FRITTATA WITH SWEET POTATOES

1 to 1½ cups sliced sweet potato, cut in thin rounds

8 pasture-raised eggs, whisked

2 cups chopped greens (arugula, kale, or spinach)

1 avocado, sliced thinly into 8 pieces

4 ounces goat cheese or Cotija cheese

¼ cup Salsa Bandera (page 62) or Green Tomatillo Salsa (page 63), optional

**SERVES 8 • PREPARATION TIME ABOUT 1 HOUR**

I love having this frittata cold one day later on a bed of greens for lunch with my Salsa Bandera or Green Tomatillo Salsa on top.

My clients make this once a week on their meal-prep days, adding in whatever veggies or meat they happen to have on hand. It's a great meal to prep ahead of time and enjoy for office lunches. I sub in zucchini in the summer and broccoli in the fall, combined with some sausage and Cheddar. This is also a really easy recipe to double and bake in a standard casserole dish for twice the deliciousness.

1. Preheat the oven to 350°F. Coat an 8-inch pie dish or circular dish with butter or oil (such as coconut) or avocado oil spray.

2. Lay the cut sweet potatoes in a thin layer in the dish bottom so that none of the dish is showing and a little up the sides as you would a crust. Bake for 18 to 20 minutes, then remove from the oven.

3. Pour in the eggs, add the greens, and then top with the avocado slices. Bake for 20 to 25 minutes longer, until the middle is no longer jiggly. Top with the cheese and salsa (if using).

# SALSAS & SAUCES

## SALSAS Y ADEREZOS

SALSA BANDERA 62

GREEN TOMATILLO SALSA 63

CHARRED RED SALSA
WITH SERRANO CHILES 64

CREAMY POBLANO
AVOCADO SALSA 65

HABANERO PEPITA
"CHEESE" SALSA 67

BONE MARROW SALSA 68

BAJA CREMA WITH LIME 70

HOMEMADE MAYO 71

GARLIC CHILE-INFUSED
EVERYDAY OIL 71

VEGAN CASHEW SPREAD 72

MEXICAN-INSPIRED
COMPOUND BUTTERS 73

Traditionally, salsa (Spanish for "sauce") is a combination of tomatoes, fresh or dried chiles, herbs, acid (such as lime juice or apple cider vinegar), and salt. Throughout Mexico, you'll see various salsas used as condiments to most dishes, served with eggs for breakfast, or simply as a side for tacos. These core ingredients can be raw, boiled, charred, or dry roasted. Salsa can be thick, chunky, or smooth. It can be burn-your-face-off spicy or so perfectly balanced that it makes you want to drink it. Once you understand these basic elements and methods, the variations are endless. In my house, we serve salsa with every single meal (including snacks). The addiction is real.

The compound that makes chile peppers hot is called capsaicin. It's in jalapeños, habaneros, cayenne peppers, and other hot chiles. It can actually cause your brain to release a chemical that makes some people feel buzzed or stoned. I first experienced this after a long day of surfing with friends five years ago. Hungry, tired, and sunburned, we gathered at a small taco shop where the *abuelita* knew me by name. There was a table to the left of her *comal* filled with more than ten different types of salsas and toppings. Pickled carrots and jalapeños, bright red onions with oregano, roasted red salsa, and the culprit—a standard-looking salsa fresca with colors that represent the Mexican flag (red tomato, green cilantro and serranos, and white onion). As we chowed down on *carne asada* tacos slathered in salsa fresca, we started to sweat and laugh. Before we knew it, we were all laughing uncontrollably. It was like we were stoned. Did the abuelita put something in our food?

Now that I know how capsaicin works, I understand that the abuelita really did put something in our food—serrano chiles! The capsaicin in the chiles sends a message to your brain that you are in pain. Our bodies instinctively try to fix the "pain" by releasing two neurotransmitters: endorphins and dopamine.

Salsa should bring flavor to your food, but it can also bring essential nutrients. Limes and raw veggies are rich in vitamin C, but unfortunately once cooked, it's gone!

My salsas are based on ancestral recipes with some tweaks for the modern cook. Every recipe has ingredients to reduce inflammation, and each ingredient is chosen to carry a specific nutrient throughout the body. Bright colors and delicious flavors send the right messages to satisfy your brain and body.

## UNDERSTANDING CHILES

There are thousands of chiles that can range in color, texture, size, and shape. They come in flavors that are sweet, hot, smoky, earthy, and even floral.

Always handle chiles with care and avoid touching your face after touching the chiles. Use rubber, latex, or plastic disposable gloves (this is the only time I will say to use anything plastic) when handling the chiles.

If they are hot but not that hot, like a jalapeño, I will usually hold the stem of the chile and use a small paring knife to scrape out and then throw the seeds in the trash or compost. The seeds have spice, but they can be bitter (especially the dried ones), so it helps if you control those flavors. Plus, removing the seeds creates an even smoothness. I only leave the seeds on my serranos and jalapeños because I am lazy and like it hot. After working with chiles, thoroughly wash your knife, cutting board, and working space to ensure you do not touch something hot and pay for it later.

### DRIED CHILES

Throughout this book, you will see that a lot of the recipes call for dried chiles, most of which you will want to dry-toast and then soak to rehydrate. I like to make sure my pantry is stocked with dried chiles because they are an easy way to add flavor to a dish. You can find them at Walmart, on Amazon, at Smart & Final, as well as in Mexican markets. I recommend ordering them online or stocking up when you see them so you have them when you want to make a recipe. Store them in mason jars or use silicone bags.

**ANAHEIM (CHILE PASADO):** These are mild in flavor and deep red in color. I like to use a mix in salsas or broth base. When fresh, they are known as green Hatch chiles.

**ANCHO:** Another name for a dried poblano, the ancho chile is mild and a bit smoky in flavor, dark purple/brown in color, and medium in size.

**ARBOL:** Nutty and mild in flavor; red, skinny, and long; great for salsas.

**CHIPOTLE IN ADOBO:** See "Keto Pantry Staples" on page 43.

**GUAJILLO:** Mild in heat, bright red with thick skins, and probably the one most people use at home.

CONTINUED

**PASILLA:** Medium heat, long, dark brown/purple color (named after raisins for its color), and spicier than the ancho.

**PEQUIN:** Very spicy, tiny balls with a great flavor. I even grind it and put it in a shaker.

## REHYDRATING DRIED CHILES

The most common varieties of dried chiles are ancho, arbol, chipotle, guajillo, pasilla, and pequin. Every recipe in this book that includes dried chiles uses them toasted and then rehydrated. To accomplish this, first discard the stems and seeds from the dried chile (I recommend using kitchen shears). Then set a *comal* or cast-iron skillet over medium heat. Dry-roast the chiles, flipping them once, until they are aromatic but not burned. Transfer the toasted chiles to a bowl and cover them with boiling water. Soak them for 10 minutes, until they look soft. Proceed with your chosen recipe.

### FRESH CHILES

**GUERO (HUNGARIAN WAX PEPPER):** *Guero* means light-skinned or blond in Spanish. These are my favorite chiles with a mild to spicy flavor depending on which one you get (see my recipe on page 135).

**HABANERO:** One of the spiciest in Mexican cooking, habaneros are orange or red and have the best flavor ever. They recently bred the hotness out to savor the flavor with none of the heat. These specialty chiles are called habanadas. When you mix them with a fat, like pepitas, they taste creamy, like queso in Habanero Pepita "Cheese" Salsa (page 67).

**JALAPEÑO:** Medium-size green chile used most commonly for guacamole and salsa fresca.

**SERRANO:** Bright green and thinner than jalapeños but with a spicier kick.

## COOKING FRESH CHILES

**BOILING:** In a large pot, cover the chiles with water and simmer until they become soft, depending on the size; this will take 10 to 15 minutes. When the skin starts to wrinkle and split, they are ready. Use this method for tomatoes, onions, and garlic, also.

**CHARRING ON AN OPEN FLAME:** Using an outdoor flame or indoor gas burner, blacken the chile by placing it directly on the flame. Use tongs to turn it until the skin is charred and blistered on all sides, about a minute on each side. You need to watch closely so that it doesn't catch on fire. If the recipe calls to remove the skin, place the charred chiles in a bowl and cover with a lid or another plate or saucepan to steam. The steam helps the skin come off easier. Next, under running water or using your hands or a towel, remove the charred parts.

**CHARRING IN THE OVEN:** You can also char or blacken chiles in the oven by placing them on a baking sheet and setting them directly beneath the broiler. Watch them closely and turn often because they can burn quickly beneath a broiler. You can get a similar char to an open flame in just a couple minutes.

**COOKING ON A CAST-IRON PAN OR COMAL:** This is called *asado*, and it means you are taking the uncooked ingredient and charring it over medium-high heat until the skin is deep brown and the inside is cooked and soft. You can leave the skin on or take it off. The skin has a lot of health benefits, so I tend to leave it on unless otherwise noted in the recipe.

**ROASTING IN THE OVEN:** This is the simplest method for achieving a deep roasted flavor. It's similar to the cast-iron method, but you don't have to turn or watch them constantly. It's as easy as setting a timer and walking away. Place your chiles on a baking sheet and roast in a 400°F oven for 20 to 40 minutes, depending on their size.

# SALSA BANDERA

4 large tomatoes (any kind is fine), chopped

1 large white onion, chopped

2 garlic cloves, minced

1 cup chopped cilantro, including stems

1 to 2 jalapeños, chopped

Juice from 1 large lime, or 1 tablespoon apple cider vinegar

2 teaspoons Celtic sea salt, plus more as needed

**MAKES 2 CUPS • PREPARATION TIME 15 MINUTES**

Bandera represents the flag of Mexico. Also known as salsa fresca, you'll recognize the colors of the Mexican flag in this finished recipe. It is fresh, easy to prepare, and great on anything. I often enjoy it on top of my Huevos Rancheros (page 53), Baja-Style Fish Tacos (page 163), and Goat Cheese Quesadillas with Hibiscus and Seasonal Veggies (page 217).

1. In a large bowl, combine the tomatoes, onion, garlic, cilantro, and jalapeño. Stir in the lime juice and salt. Toss until thoroughly combined, adding more salt if you wish. Store in the fridge for up to 5 days.

## FERMENTED VERSION

4 large tomatoes, chopped

1 large white onion, chopped

2 cloves garlic, minced

1 cup chopped cilantro, including stems

1 to 2 jalapeños, chopped

Juice from 1 large lime, or 1 tablespoon apple cider vinegar

1 to 2 teaspoons kosher salt

**MAKES 2 CUPS • PREPARATION TIME 4 DAYS, 15 MINUTES ACTIVE TIME**

We can thank the good bacteria buzzing through fermented foods for better digestion and absorption of nutrients. The peppers taste tangier, the garlic is more intense, and the tomatoes taste sweeter.

1. In a large bowl, combine the tomatoes, onion, garlic, cilantro, and jalapeño. Stir in the lime juice and 1 teaspoon of the salt. Toss until thoroughly combined, adding more salt if you wish. You can also blend the salsa at this stage if you prefer a smoother consistency.

2. Pour the prepared salsa into two large, clean mason jars. Make sure you press the mixture down into the jar so the juices cover the salsa. Be sure to leave some room at the top for proper fermentation. Cap loosely.

3. Place the salsa in a cool, dark spot in the pantry. Let it sit for 2 to 3 days. You should start to see tiny bubbles. This is a good sign that the salsa is fermenting.

4. After 4 days, transfer the jars to the fridge. The colder temperature slows the fermentation process. Stir or shake the mason jars each day so that surface mold doesn't develop. The salsa will last for up to 2 months in the fridge.

# GREEN TOMATILLO SALSA

**MAKES 3½ CUPS • PREPARATION TIME 30 MINUTES**

*Tomatillo* means "little tomato" in Spanish. Small, firm, and green with a lantern-type paper covering, they're not easily recognized in the produce aisle and are often missed. When roasted, the firm acidic meat of the tomatillo transforms into a sticky-sweet caramel you'll want to serve with everything. But note the naturally occurring sugars in the salsa are better absorbed in our bodies by adding a healthy fat such as MCT or avocado oil. Tomatillos are packed with many vitamins, specifically vitamin C, and the mineral manganese. They also contain fourteen types of phytochemical compounds called withanolides that are antibacterial and cancer fighting.

Try blending an avocado in with the onion and garlic for a creamier texture, or serve the salsa with chopped avocado on the side.

10 to 12 tomatillos, rinsed, husks removed

2 to 3 serrano chiles

½ small white onion, peeled

2 garlic cloves, skin on

1 tablespoon kosher salt

2 tablespoons MCT oil or avocado oil

¼ cup freshly squeezed lime juice

1 cup coarsely chopped cilantro, including stems

1. Preheat the oven to 400°F. Arrange the whole tomatillos, chiles, onion, and garlic on a baking sheet. Roast in the oven for 20 minutes, until golden brown, turning over when halfway through the roasting time.

2. Remove the baking sheet from the oven and allow to cool slightly. Carefully remove the stems from the chiles and tomatillos and transfer the chiles and tomatillos to a blender along with the onion and garlic. Add the salt and MCT oil and blend on high until the mixture is well combined. Add the lime juice and cilantro and blend again. Store in the fridge for up to 5 days. Serve the salsa at room temperature.

## BAJA BOILED VERSION

I commonly see the boiled version of this recipe in Baja. It's just as easy and yields a completely different flavor. Instead of roasting, boil the tomatillos, chiles, onion, and garlic in a medium saucepan for 8 to 10 minutes, until soft. Strain and transfer to a blender with the remaining ingredients. Blend until smooth.

# CHARRED RED SALSA WITH SERRANO CHILES

6 medium tomatoes
(such as Roma)

6 to 8 serrano chiles,
seeds removed

½ white onion, peeled

2 garlic cloves, peeled

½ bunch cilantro, coarsely
chopped

1 tablespoon kosher salt,
plus more as needed

**MAKES 1½ CUPS • PREPARATION TIME 30 MINUTES**

This salsa is so flavorful, you'll want to drink it. I love it boiled or roasted and always have a jar on hand. In most kitchens, this is a staple for topping carne asada, chicken, eggs, and quesadillas.

1.  Char the tomatoes, chiles, and onion on a *comal* or cast-iron skillet for 15 to 20 minutes, turning over often. They will be brown and almost burnt when ready. Transfer to a blender along with the garlic and blend until chunky or smooth, depending on your preference. Add the cilantro and pulse, then add the salt and pulse again. Season with additional salt if you wish. Store in the fridge for up to 5 days.

## BOILED VERSION

Place the tomatoes, chiles, and onion in a large stockpot and top with water. Bring to a boil and cook until tender, about 10 minutes. (The tomatoes should look wilted when ready.) Drain the water. Transfer all to a blender along with the raw garlic and blend until smooth. Pulse in the cilantro and salt at the end. Some people like to add more salt. It's really up to your taste.

# CREAMY POBLANO AVOCADO SALSA

**MAKES 3 CUPS • PREPARATION TIME 35 MINUTES**

Sweet poblanos and creamy avocado balance the kick from jalapeños, creating a punchy thick topping great for Grilled Flank Steak Arrachera (page 175), Whole Fish, Camp-Style (page 164), or Goat Cheese Frittata with Sweet Potatoes (page 54).

2 poblano or Anaheim chiles

1 to 2 jalapeños

3 garlic cloves, peeled

½ cup freshly squeezed lime juice

1 bunch cilantro, including stems, coarsely chopped

2 avocados

½ cup avocado oil

Sea salt

1. Preheat the oven to 450°F. Place the poblanos and jalapeños on a baking sheet and roast for 25 minutes, turning halfway through the roasting time. They should be charred. Remove the baking sheet from the oven and allow the chiles to cool slightly before carefully removing their stems. (If you have any inflammation issues, you can sweat and peel the poblano skin. See method on page 61.)

2. Place the whole roasted poblanos and jalapeños, the garlic, and lime juice in a blender and blend until smooth. Add the cilantro and avocados and blend until smooth. Slowly add the avocado oil through the top of the blender while blending. If the consistency is too thick, add filtered water 1 tablespoon at a time until the desired consistency is reached. Season with salt to your liking. Store in the fridge for up to 5 days

**NOTE** You can make this recipe more authentic (how most Mexicans are making it at home) by cooking the poblanos and jalapeños straight on the *comal* or cast iron (see page 61). It will be a bit smoky and more time consuming, but the charred flavor profile tastes just like what you would find at a taco stand on the streets of Mexico.

# HABANERO PEPITA "CHEESE" SALSA

**MAKES 1½ CUPS • PREPARATION TIME 30 MINUTES**

This recipe came about because I loved the taste of habaneros but could never make anything that wasn't so dang *caliente*. I read that if you add a fat, it helps to tone down the spice. I call this the habanero "cheese" salsa because so many people swear there is cheese in it. Pumpkin seeds, also known as pepitas, combined with the roasted garlic create a natural cheesy flavor. It's great for a dip, on tacos, or even on nachos.

The pepitas contain amazing health-enhancing nutrients from magnesium, protein, niacin, and zinc to its high concentration of essential fatty acids.

2 to 3 habanero chiles

5 medium tomatoes (any kind is fine), skin on

½ white onion, skin on

5 garlic cloves, skin on

1 cup raw pepitas, soaked (see Note)

1 cup cold pressed olive oil

Sea salt

1. Preheat the oven to 400°F. Line a baking sheet with parchment paper. Lay the habaneros, tomatoes, onion, and garlic on the prepared baking sheet. Roast for about 20 minutes, turning over halfway through the roasting time. (You want them to be golden brown, not burnt.)

2. Meanwhile, in a cast iron skillet over medium heat lightly toast the soaked pepitas until golden brown and fragrant, 4 to 5 minutes. Once you smell them, they are done.

3. Remove the stems from the roasted habaneros, taking care not to touch any seeds with your hands. Remove the skin from the onion and garlic.

4. Place the roasted ingredients in a food processor or blender and blend well. Blend again on slow speed, adding the olive oil until emulsified. Season with salt. Store in the fridge for up to 5 days.

**NOTE** Soaking works to eliminate nutritional inhibitors and natural occurring toxins found in nuts, grains, and seeds. The process reduces phytic acid, enzyme inhibitors, and tannins, while also increasing bioavailability, vitamins, and minerals. Soaking helps with absorption, making proteins readily available, and easing your digestion.

Make sure everything is covered by 2 inches of cold filtered water. Add kosher salt (about 1 tablespoon to 4 cups of nuts, grains, or seeds) and soak for 7 to 12 hours. Rinse well and use soaked, or dehydrate (12 hours at 150 degrees in a dehydrator) for crunch! For storing, keep in glass jars in the fridge if you live in a warm area. Avoid buying nuts in bulk as they can become rancid.

# BONE MARROW SALSA

2 dried ancho or guajillo
chiles

1 pound marrow bones
(about 2 bones)

Pinch of sea salt

1 garlic clove, skin on

½ white onion, skin on

2 tomatoes (any kind is fine)

Kosher salt and coarse
black pepper

**MAKES 1 CUP • PREPARATION TIME 30 MINUTES**

Although a departure from the typical salsa recipes we see today, our ancestors were known to use every scrap of the animal, leaving nothing to waste—even down to the bone marrow. This ingredient may be part of the reason our ancestors lived with less ailments and didn't suffer from the same diseases experienced by our generation. Bone marrow is incredibly nutrient dense and is a significant source of the hormone adiponectin, which helps to maintain insulin sensitivity and break down fat, and has been linked to a decreased risk of cardiovascular disease, diabetes, and obesity-associated cancers. This salsa is my spin on the traditional method.

1. Cook the dried chiles on a cast-iron skillet or *comal* (see the method on page 61). Meanwhile, bring 4 cups of water to a boil. Transfer the toasted chiles to a large bowl along with the marrow bones. Cover the chiles and bones with the boiling water, add the sea salt, and allow to soak for 15 minutes.

2. While the chiles and bones soak, use the same pan to dry-roast the garlic, onion, and tomatoes over medium heat until blistered, 6 to 8 minutes. Remove the skin from the onion and garlic. Transfer the soaked chiles to a blender along with the dry-roasted garlic, onion, tomato, and ¼ cup of the soaking liquid. Blend until smooth, then season with salt and pepper.

3. Use a butter knife to remove the marrow from the bones and transfer it to the pan. Cook the marrow over medium-low heat for 5 minutes, seasoning with salt and pepper. Add the blended salsa mixture to the pan and cook for 5 to 7 minutes, until mixed thoroughly. Let cool. Store in fridge for up to 5 days.

**NOTE** Save the used marrow bones in your freezer to add to your bone broth on page 120.

# BAJA CREMA WITH LIME

1½ cups mayonnaise, full-fat Greek-style yogurt, or sour cream

3 to 4 tablespoons freshly squeezed lime juice

Zest from 1 lime (about 1 teaspoon)

½ teaspoon kosher salt, plus more as needed

¼ cup water

**ADDITIONS**

Raw or caramelized shallots; chopped cilantro, chives, parsley, or herb of choice; chopped green onions; fresh or dried epazote, chili powder, chipotle powder, ground cumin, or turmeric powder

**MAKES 2 CUPS • PREPARATION TIME 10 MINUTES**

Classic homemade crema is one of two things: mayo with lime juice or buttermilk mixed with heavy cream to create a kind of sour cream. It is traditionally served on sopes, fish tacos, and tostadas. To be completely honest, I've always hated mayo. The thought of dairy-based crema sitting out in a hot taco shop was always gross to me until I took a food tour in San Miguel de Allende. I tasted cremas there that were fresh and bright and added amazing depth of flavor to simple fish tacos. I came home and developed this recipe, and now we use it on everything.

Store-bought mayos are packed with chemicals, hydrogenated oils, and sugar. I'm calling for high-quality store-bought mayo here, but if you want to be a rock star and make your own, see the recipe on the facing page. Homemade mayo should be made of egg yolks, clean oil, lemon juice, and your favorite spices. Otherwise, organic mayo, full-fat Greek-Style yogurt, or organic sour cream will do the trick.

1. Whisk together the mayonnaise, lime juice, lime zest, and salt. Add the water and continue to whisk until everything is combined (you can add more water to thin to your liking). You can also shake everything together in a mason jar. Fold in any additions (if using). Season with more salt if you so desire. Store in the fridge for 3 to 5 days.

# HOMEMADE MAYO

**MAKES 1 CUP • PREPARATION TIME 15 MINUTES**

The key to making mayo thick and not having to do much work is using an immersion or hand blender and slowly adding the oil.

2 pasture-raised egg yolks

1 teaspoon freshly squeezed lemon juice

½ teaspoon Dijon mustard

½ teaspoon sea salt

1 cup olive oil or avocado oil

1. In a blender, food processor, or using an immersion blender set to low, combine the egg yolks, lemon juice, mustard, and sea salt. Slowly add the oil in a constant stream while blending. This process should take about 2 minutes. Blend until the mixture is emulsified and the desired consistency is reached. The mayo will last in the fridge for 1 week.

# GARLIC CHILE-INFUSED EVERYDAY OIL

**MAKES 2 CUPS • PREPARATION TIME 2 HOURS 15 MINUTES**

In order to reap all the benefits of keto, you must add extra oils to your cooked dishes or on top of raw veggies. This recipe fills your house with an incredible aroma. Because this recipe is cooked at 300°F for a controlled, low heat, it is safe and will not harm the unstable oil. Find out more about oils on page 33. If you want to keep the garlic, you can either put it in the container with the oil or pulse it into salad dressings. What is better than oily roasted garlic?

4 garlic heads

3 sprigs oregano, or 2 teaspoons dried oregano

10 to 15 dried chiles de arbol

1 to 2 tablespoons dried chile pequin (optional)

1 cup MCT oil

1 cup extra-virgin olive oil, plus more as needed

1. Preheat the oven to 300°F. In a 10-inch cast-iron skillet or heavy Dutch oven, place the garlic, oregano, and chiles. Pour in both oils to cover the garlic, adding more olive oil if necessary. Cover with the lid. Roast in the oven for 2 hours and then let cool completely.

2. Once cooled, strain the oil and use a funnel to either pour it into a reusable bottle or glass mason jar. Oil is best stored in the fridge to keep its freshness and will last for months.

# VEGAN CASHEW SPREAD

1 cup raw cashews

¼ teaspoon kosher salt, plus more as needed

2 to 3 tablespoons freshly squeezed lime juice

1 tablespoon apple cider vinegar

¼ cup nutritional yeast

¼ teaspoon turmeric powder

½ teaspoon smoked paprika

2 garlic cloves, peeled

**MAKES 1 CUP • PREPARATION TIME 10 MINUTES, PLUS 6 TO 12 HOURS OF SOAKING**

Nuts are so versatile. I've been using them more than ever since playing around with dairy-free alternatives. I find that dairy impacts many of my clients (especially those with gut issues). If you have gut issues, do not worry. I had a ton of gut issues years ago, have healed myself, and am here to help others do the same. For now, if dairy isn't your friend, stick to this recipe.

This is a dairy-free alternative to a cheese sauce or dip. It has an amazing creamy, cheesy texture that people go crazy for. Soaking the nuts makes it that much creamier (see Note on page 67). You can also serve this as a dairy-free *crema* by thinning it out with more water.

1. In a large bowl, cover the cashews with cold filtered water and the salt. Make sure the cashews are covered by 2 inches of water. Top with a dish towel and leave to soak for a minimum of 6 hours, or overnight. The cashews will soak up a ton of water, so make sure your bowl is big enough. Drain and rinse the soaked nuts to remove the salt taste.

2. Place the soaked cashews in a blender or food processor and add the lime juice, apple cider vinegar, nutritional yeast, turmeric, paprika, garlic, and enough fresh water to just cover the cashews. Blend until the mixture is smooth. If you want to use this as a crema, stir in hot water until the desired consistency is achieved. Season with more salt. Store in the fridge for 3 to 5 days.

**NOTE** If you want to spice it up, add 1 to 2 canned chipotles in adobo sauce plus 2 teaspoons of sauce from the can. You can also add ½ teaspoon chili powder.

# MEXICAN-INSPIRED COMPOUND BUTTERS

**MAKES ¾ CUP • PREPARATION TIME 30 MINUTES**

If you've never made compound butter before, you are in for a treat. Compound butter is just a fancy add-on to your normal butter. Mixing butter with fresh herbs, spices, citrus, and more is a fantastic way to bring bold flavors and aromas to the table. It elevates a dish and makes cooking that much more delish. Plus, if you prep it ahead of time, it's simple to add to any meal or recipe.

I've included a few of my favorite blends on the following pages, but don't be shy about using what you have on hand. Do you have extra spices or fresh herbs sitting around or about to go bad? Or perhaps some extra bacon? Adding these elements to butter will add flavor and make it look so great. Try it on barbecued oysters, slathered on your steak, baked inside the flesh of your whole fish, or thrown in on a weeknight veggie sauté and you will be so, so satisfied.

When buying butter, always choose unsalted, high-quality butter. It should be grass-fed and closer to yellow than white with a high-fat content. Remember: The better the quality, the better the taste and the health benefits. I like European butter, which has a higher fat content. Kerrygold and Vital Farms butters are easy to find at most large grocery stores and won't break the bank.

**CONTINUED**

**MORINGA BACON PARSLEY BUTTER** Sauté with this butter with eggs or add to the Ramekin-Baked Eggs on page 52. Pack on top of grilled oysters or add to sautéed greens.

**MUSHROOM SPICED BUTTER** This is so good in your morning high-fat coffee or tea (see pages 48 and 49). Having this made ahead of time also saves you a couple of extra steps in the morning. By using this in your high-fat drink, you start your day with proper fat-burning, brain-boosting fuel. Oh, and I also love it on my pork chops (see page 176).

**ANCHO AVOCADO BUTTER** This might be my favorite of all the compound butter recipes. I like to serve it as an appetizer to dip radishes or carrots. Try it stuffed inside Whole Fish, Camp-Style (page 164) or on top of Grilled Flank Steak Arrachera (page 175).

**LIME PEPITA BUTTER** The crunch from the pepitas along with the spice factor can go on anything. Try it on roast chicken (see page 170) or roasted cauliflower and broccoli (see page 139).

**GARLIC HERB BUTTER** Depending on what's in season, you can make this recipe with two ingredients: garlic and cilantro. Or you can mix in a ton of herbs such as parsley, chives, tarragon, basil, thyme, green onion, rosemary, and epazote. I love nutritional yeast because it adds a cheesy component, but you can totally leave it out if you don't want that flavor. Try this butter on Coconut Tortillas with Lard (page 209).

> **NOTE** If you are dairy-free, you can substitute the butter with ghee. For a superfood boost, add zest, nuts, roasted garlic, roasted jalapeño, or spices to your butter of choice.

## MORINGA BACON PARSLEY BUTTER

8 tablespoons butter, at room temperature

½ teaspoon kosher salt

1 tablespoon moringa powder

6 tablespoons chopped cooked bacon

3 teaspoons minced parsley

## MUSHROOM SPICED BUTTER

8 tablespoons butter, at room temperature

1½ tablespoons maca powder

1½ tablespoons powdered mushroom adaptogens of choice (chaga, reishi, and so on)

1½ tablespoons cinnamon

10 to 15 drops liquid stevia, or 1 teaspoon monk fruit sugar (optional)

## ANCHO AVOCADO BUTTER

8 tablespoons butter, at room temperature

½ teaspoon kosher salt

8 to 10 ounces avocado (about ½ avocado)

2 toasted rehydrated ancho chiles (see page 60), minced

1 teaspoon minced roasted garlic

2 teaspoons lime zest

1 tablespoon freshly squeezed lime juice

2 teaspoons ground cumin

Freshly ground black pepper

## LIME PEPITA BUTTER

8 tablespoons butter, at room temperature

½ teaspoon kosher salt

1 tablespoon minced jalapeño

Zest from 1 lime

1 tablespoon freshly squeezed lime juice

2 tablespoons minced cilantro

1 teaspoon turmeric powder

1 to 2 tablespoons roughly chopped pepitas

## GARLIC HERB BUTTER

8 tablespoons butter, at room temperature

½ teaspoon kosher salt

½ tablespoon white wine vinegar

1 to 2 tablespoons minced garlic, or 1 teaspoon garlic powder

4 tablespoons chopped herbs of choice (see facing page)

1 tablespoon nutritional yeast

1. In a large bowl or food processor, combine all the ingredients, mixing well until evenly combined. I like to smash with a fork. Place on a piece of parchment paper and roll tightly like a burrito. Twist the ends to seal well. If you just want to use it in a recipe, go for it. Refrigerate at least 1 hour if you want medallions. You can store it in your fridge for up to 1 week or in the freezer for up to 2 months.

# SNACKS & APPETIZERS

## BOTANAS Y APERITIVOS

I was the queen of snacking until I started my keto journey four years ago. If you're anything like I was, you probably need to eat every couple hours to not be hangry. Am I right? Well, by the end of this book, I am going to change that for you. Your brain and hunger should not rule your life, mood, and personality. Of course, there are still days when I need a little snack, usually when I haven't had my high-fat beverage in the morning (see page 46). I created these dishes more as appetizers, but they make great snacks, too!

## ALTERNATIVE KETO WRAPS TO USE AS TORTILLAS, TOSTADAS, AND CHIPS

- Jicama
- Neck of butternut squash (blanched in boiling water for 10 seconds)
- Roasted or blanched nopal
- Butterhead lettuce
- Iceberg lettuce
- Cabbage (purple, green, and savoy)
- Coconut Tortillas with Lard (page 209)
- Crispy Cheese Taco Shells (facing page)

# CRISPY CHEESE TACO SHELLS

**MAKES 6 SHELLS • PREPARATION TIME 15 MINUTES**

This is not your average taco shell. It's actually made with cheese and is easier to make than a homemade tortilla. When I was growing up, my mom went to a fancy cooking school in Italy. When she came home, she would make these in a Parmesan version and form them into bowls topped with her amazing Caesar salad. Once you get the hang of how easy it is to form these crispy cheese shells, you can lay them flat into tostadas, crumble into croutons, or form into bowls!

When selecting your cheese, make sure to read the package. Some preshredded cheese contains additives and fillers to make sure the cheese does not melt or harden in the bag.

2 cups shredded Cheddar cheese

½ teaspoon chili powder, garlic powder, or your favorite spice mix

½ teaspoon turmeric powder

1. Preheat the oven to 375°F. Line a large baking sheet with parchment paper. In a medium bowl, toss the shredded cheese with the chili or garlic powder (or both) and turmeric.

2. Arrange ⅓ cup of the cheese mixture in circles on the baking sheet and spread evenly. It is important to have the same size circles (thickness and diameter) so that they cook evenly. You can use an ice cream scoop or measuring cup to keep it consistent.

3. Bake for 8 to 10 minutes, or until little holes have appeared in the surface and the edges have just turned golden brown. While they are baking, prep your cups and spoon for shaping the taco shells (hot out of the oven) by placing two cups facing down with a wooden spoon balanced in between. Remove the baking sheet from the oven and let cool for just 1 minute. Working in batches, use a spatula to lift each taco shell and hang it over the spoon to create a taco shell shape. Let them cool and harden for 5 minutes. It's important to work quickly, so the shells don't harden before you can form them. Serve immediately as these don't keep for longer than 1 to 2 days.

**NOTE** Crush ½ cup pasture-raised pork rinds (I like to use Epic brand) into the cheese during step 1 for an added heavenly crunch. You can also sprinkle in fresh herbs, which will make the shells very pretty.

# MEXICAN CRUDITÉ

1 cup jicama, cut into
¼-inch-thin sticks

4 carrots, cut into
¼-inch-thin sticks

1 bunch radish (I like using
watermelon radish), halved

5 small cucumbers,
quartered (if using the big
ones, remove the seeds)

**DRESSINGS**

Vegan Cashew Spread
(page 72)

Cilantro Yogurt Dressing
(page 108)

**ADDITIONS**

½ cup olives

½ cup Taco-Spiced Mixed
Nuts (page 83)

3 limes, quartered

Pickled Fennel (page 146)

Stuffed Crunchy Squash
Blossoms (page 136)

Taqueria-Style Pickled
Jalapeños and Carrots
(page 148)

**SERVES 8 TO 10 • PREPARATION TIME 25 MINUTES**

This is perfect for when you're hosting friends, and it always looks so
pretty. You can make it seasonal by adding tomatoes and stuffed squash
blossoms in the summer and roasted winter squash and cauliflower in
the colder months. This is also my favorite dish to bring to parties because
you never know what kind of food they will be serving and at least this
way you know you brought something healthy to satisfy and nourish you.
Cut and refrigerate the veggies a couple of hours in advance.

1. Lay the vegetables out on a large cheese board or platter. Arrange with
   dressings and any other additions, such as olives or nuts, in small bowls to
   give it an inviting feel. Serve immediately.

# TACO-SPICED MIXED NUTS

**SERVES 4 • PREPARATION TIME 30 MINUTES, PLUS SOAKING**

This is one of those recipes that people always ask for after they taste it. I tend to put it out for guests or toss it in my salad for extra depth and crunch. Ideally, all of the nuts should be soaked for best absorption and proper digestion. Before you make this, check out my thoughts on why you should be soaking your nuts on page 67.

⅔ cup raw macadamia nuts

⅔ cup raw pecans

⅔ cup raw walnuts

⅔ cup raw pepitas

1 teaspoon chili powder

½ teaspoon turmeric powder

½ teaspoon ground cumin

½ teaspoon freshly ground black pepper

1 teaspoon kosher salt

1 tablespoon MCT oil or olive oil

1. Preheat the oven to 275°F and line a baking sheet with parchment paper. Place the macadamia nuts, pecans, walnuts, and pepitas in a single layer on the baking sheet and roast for 25 to 30 minutes, mixing halfway through the roasting time. You can also roast on the stovetop in a cast-iron skillet over low to medium heat. (This process usually takes 8 to 10 minutes on the stove, but watch closely so they do not burn.) You know they are done when you can smell the nuts and they become golden on the outside.

2. Remove the baking sheet from the oven and place the mixture in a bowl. Toss them with the chili powder, turmeric, cumin, black pepper, salt, and oil to evenly coat.

3. Allow the nuts to cool before serving. Store them in an airtight glass container or mason jar. They will last for 1 month in the fridge or 1 week on your counter.

**NOTE** Buy raw nuts and switch out any nuts suggested above for your favorites (almonds, cashews, pistachios) with the exception of peanuts. Peanuts are actually legumes and have more of the bad inflammatory omega-6s.

# SMOKED FISH DIP ON SWEET POTATO CROSTINIS

2 tablespoons MCT oil or avocado oil

1 teaspoon turmeric powder

1 teaspoon paprika or chili powder

½ teaspoon kosher salt, plus more as needed

½ teaspoon freshly ground black pepper, plus more as needed

2 small sweet potatoes, sliced into ¼-inch rounds (preferably with a mandoline)

1 pound skinned and flaked smoked whitefish, salmon, cod, yellowtail (stick to small fish if possible), or canned wild fish

½ cup Greek-style yogurt, coconut cream, or mayonnaise

2 tablespoons stone-ground mustard

1 teaspoon apple cider vinegar

1 tablespoon lime zest

Juice from 1 lime

¼ cup finely sliced green onions, both white and green parts

¼ cup chopped cilantro

½ jalapeño, finely chopped or 4 or 5 pickled jalapeño slices (see page 148)

**SERVES 8 TO 10 • PREPARATION TIME 25 MINUTES**

This smoked fish dip is super-versatile and can be made with whatever herbs and fish you happen to have on hand. Do not be afraid of smoked fish; once you add these yummy ingredients, it is not stinky at all. I promise it will become your favorite new party snack.

1. Preheat the oven to 400°F and line a baking sheet with parchment paper. In a large bowl, mix together the oil, turmeric, paprika, salt, and pepper. Add the sliced sweet potatoes and toss to coat evenly. Arrange the sweet potato slices on the lined baking sheet and roast until they are golden brown and crisp, 18 to 20 minutes. Let them come to room temperature.

2. In a large mixing bowl, combine the fish with the yogurt, mustard, and vinegar. Add the lime zest, lime juice, and green onions. Add salt and pepper to taste. If you want a smooth consistency, whirl it in a food processor or use an immersion blender. You can also leave it chunky.

3. Using a teaspoon, scoop the fish dip on top of each toasted sweet potato. Top with the cilantro and jalapeño. You can also serve it as a do-it-yourself with the roasted sweet potatoes around a bowl of dip.

**NOTE** Sometimes I will substitute ricotta or a good mayo for half of the Greek-style yogurt. I find that two different creamy white things blended together create a more complex flavor.

# NOURISHING ANCESTRAL LIVER PÂTÉ WITH GHEE

**SERVES 6 TO 8 • PREPARATION TIME 35 MINUTES**

Not only is liver a good-for-you ancestral superfood, it's also cheap to make and so delicious. You can smear it on seed crackers or thinly sliced cucumbers with my pickled red onions (see page 147). Liver is one of the most nutrient-dense foods in the world. It's rich in protein, fat-soluble vitamins A, D, E, and K, $B_{12}$, trace minerals, purines, and antioxidants like $CoQ_{10}$. It boosts our body's phosphorus, zinc, iron, riboflavin, and folate. And quality matters, so make sure to always buy the highest-quality liver available.

1 pound pasture-raised chicken livers

8 tablespoons ghee or grass-fed butter

2 shallots, finely minced

2 garlic cloves, finely minced

2 tablespoons apple cider vinegar or freshly squeezed lime juice

¼ cup water

4 tablespoons coconut cream or heavy cream (if not dairy-free)

2 tablespoons MCT oil

1 teaspoon sea salt

½ teaspoon freshly ground black pepper

½ teaspoon nutmeg

1. Prepare the chicken livers by using kitchen shears or a small knife to trim off any discolored parts, excess fat, veins, and connective tissues (the stringy bits). This step ensures a creamy pâté consistency at the end. Rinse the livers, pat them dry with a paper towel, and slice thinly.

2. Heat a medium pan over medium-low heat. Use about 1 tablespoon of the ghee to grease the pan. Add the shallots and cook until they have softened but not browned, approximately 3 minutes. Add the garlic for the last minute, making sure not to burn it. Add the vinegar and cook until most of the liquid has evaporated, 3 to 5 minutes. Transfer the shallots, garlic, and pan sauce to a food processor.

3. Grease the pan with 4 tablespoons of ghee so that the livers don't dry out. Add the water and the livers and sauté just until they are cooked through and no longer pink on the inside, about 5 minutes. Do not overcook them. Transfer the contents of the pan to the food processor.

4. Pulse the livers with the shallot-garlic mixture, adding the remaining ghee, 1 tablespoon at a time, until all of the ghee has been incorporated and the pâté is very smooth, about 5 minutes (scrape the sides down as necessary). Add in the coconut cream, MCT oil, salt, pepper, and nutmeg. Process until well combined; it should be very smooth.

5. Transfer the chicken liver mixture into ramekins or other serving dishes and level the surface using a small spoon or spatula. Cover and chill the pâté for at least 2 hours or overnight, so the flavors can set and come together, before serving.

# BAKED QUESO WITH OREGANO AND GARLIC

10 ounces fresh cheese, such as Cotija, queso panela, Oaxacan, or goat cheese, roughly cubed

2 tablespoons fresh oregano, chopped and stems removed, or 1 teaspoon dried oregano

6 garlic cloves, peeled

1 teaspoon Himalayan salt

1 teaspoon freshly cracked black pepper

1 tablespoon lime zest

2 tablespoons olive oil or MCT oil

2 to 3 tablespoons minced jalapeños or chiles of any kind (optional)

Crackers, tortilla chips (see page 213), or veggies for dipping

**SERVES 4 TO 6 • PREPARATION TIME 30 MINUTES**

There's nothing like homemade cheese. In southern Baja, where I spend a lot of time, we wait anxiously for the rancheros to come into town for supplies, bearing fresh cheese made from the milk of their goats, sheep, and cows. Sometimes we eat it with cured meats, nuts, olives, and crackers. But most of the time, we just scarf it down before we have time to grab any other ingredients. One colder night, I decided to bake it with herbs.

1. Preheat the broiler and position the oven rack 5 inches from the heat. Place the cheese in an oven-safe dish. I love using my cast-iron skillet for this.

2. In a large bowl, mix together the oregano, garlic, salt, pepper, lime zest, oil, and chiles (if using). Distribute the mixture evenly over the cheese.

3. Place the pan under the broiler for 10 to 15 minutes, checking on it occasionally. You know it's ready when the cheese is melted, bubbling, and beginning to brown. Serve the baked queso family-style out of the oven with crackers, tortilla chips, or fresh veggies.

NOTE If you can't find a fresh Mexican cheese you can use fontina, mozzarella, or Cheddar.

# PROBIOTIC GUACAMOLE

**MAKES 2 CUPS • PREPARATION TIME 25 MINUTES**

Who doesn't love a good guac? I first learned this recipe while working at Rancho La Puerta's cooking school and quickly started using it for all my parents who wanted to sneak more veggies and healthy fats into their kids' meals. Over the years, I've made it my own by upping the fat, incorporating fermented foods for their probiotics, and adding superfoods such as moringa powder, chia seeds, and collagen peptides. Make sure you scrape out all the avocado connected to the skin. The flesh closest to the skin is actually the most nutrient-dense part! The lime juice in this recipe keeps the guacamole from turning brown. Serve this with Mushroom Vegetarian Tostada with all the Toppings (page 224) or Tinga Tomato-Chile Stewed Chicken (page 173).

1 cup frozen green peas, thawed, or shelled edamame or broccoli florets

2 medium avocados

1 jalapeño or serrano chile, minced

¼ cup chopped red onions

¼ cup chopped cilantro

1 teaspoon minced garlic

2 tablespoons chopped sauerkraut

2 tablespoons sauerkraut brine

½ teaspoon ground cumin

3 tablespoons freshly squeezed lime juice

1 to 2 tablespoons MCT oil (optional)

Himalayan salt

Dash of cayenne pepper (optional)

1. In a small saucepan, cook the peas in boiling water for 2 to 3 minutes. Drain and leave to cool slightly.

2. In a blender or food processor, process the peas until smooth. (You can add a splash of water or lime juice to help blend if you are having trouble.) In a medium bowl, mash the avocados with a fork. Stir in the chile, red onions, cilantro, garlic, sauerkraut and sauerkraut brine, cumin, lime juice, and MCT oil (if using). Stir in the blended veggies. Add salt to taste and cayenne pepper, if using.

**NOTE** This can be made up to 3 hours ahead and refrigerated. I like to serve this in a molcajete for parties or for having friends over.

# PADRÓN PEPPERS WITH BONITO FLAKES

1 pound Padrón or shishito peppers (18 to 20 peppers)

2 to 3 tablespoons high-heat oil, such as avocado oil or sesame oil

Zest and juice of 1 lime

½ teaspoon flaky sea salt, such as Maldon

1 tablespoon bonito flakes

**SERVES 5 • PREPARATION TIME 15 MINUTES**

Most Padrón chiles are mild, but one out of ten has a little kick, and it's always fun to see who gets the hot one. Think of it as a little chile Russian roulette, making eating that much more exciting. Japanese shishitos are a fine alternative, and both they and Spanish Padrón peppers are usually available in health food stores, Asian stores, and farmers' markets. The razor-thin bonito flakes "dance" on top of the peppers to get the party started.

1. Heat a heavy pan to medium-high heat. It's best to use a cast-iron skillet or cook outside on the grill with a grill pan or vegetable rack. The charring of the peppers tends to create smoke.

2. Toss the peppers with the oil and place in the hot skillet. Turn the heat to high and cook, tossing and turning frequently, for 5 to 7 minutes, until well charred or blistered.

3. Transfer the peppers to a medium bowl and toss with the lime zest and juice and flaky sea salt. Top with the bonito flakes before serving. Grab the peppers by their stems and eat the whole thing minus the stem. They disappear fast.

NOTE *Charring* refers to blistering the outermost layer at high heat for a short amount of time. This makes for a bolder smoky flavor. See page 61 for methods.

# CAULIFLOWER SOPES

**SERVES 6 • PREPARATION TIME 45 MINUTES**

*Sopes* are like smaller, thicker corn tortillas. Their density makes them the perfect vehicle for all kinds of proteins and toppings. Cauliflower is packed with vitamin K, vitamin C, B vitamins, and beta-carotene, it's also anti-inflammatory and helps with detoxification and digestion. I usually top the *sopes* with shredded meat, smoked fish, veggies, and cheese and then broil for a couple of minutes.

1 head cauliflower, cut into chunks, or 3 cups store-bought pre-riced cauliflower

Avocado oil or coconut oil for greasing pan and frying sopes

1 pasture-raised egg, whisked

¼ cup cassava flour or almond flour

½ teaspoon salt

½ teaspoon freshly ground black pepper

1. Preheat the oven to 375°F. If you are making cauliflower rice from scratch, place the chunked cauliflower in a food processor and pulse until really fine (finer than rice). If using store-bought cauliflower rice, I recommend putting it in the food processor as well to get it as fine as possible.

2. Steam the riced cauliflower in a steamer basket over medium-low heat for 5 to 6 minutes to cook through and get the moisture to release. Let the cauliflower cool so that it is not too hot to handle.

3. Place the cooled steamed cauliflower rice in a thin dish towel or cheesecloth and squeeze out as much liquid as possible. Squeeze some more to make sure you really have removed as much liquid as you can (otherwise, you'll have soggy sopes). Lightly grease a parchment paper–lined baking sheet with a little avocado oil or coconut oil so the sopes do not stick.

4. In a large bowl, whisk together the cauliflower rice, egg, flour, salt, and pepper until the mixture is thoroughly combined. Use your hands to roll the mixture into six balls. The batter will feel loose but will come together as you form the sopes. Arrange the balls on the prepared baking sheet and flatten into circles with thick, raised edges, like pizza (I like to use a spoon to form them).

5. Bake for 12 minutes. Remove the baking sheet from oven and use a spatula to flip the sopes. Bake them for another 3 to 5 minutes. Take them out and place on a cooling rack for 10 minutes.

6. Just before serving, heat a cast-iron or stainless-steel skillet and a little bit of avocado oil. Working one or two at a time, heat each sope in the pan until golden brown and crispy, adding more oil as needed. Serve immediately.

# SALADS & DRESSINGS

## ENSALADAS Y VINAGRETAS

I grew up in a household where we always had some sort of salad at both lunch and dinner. My dad owned restaurants in the 1990s, and his restaurants were some of the first in San Diego to introduce a salad bar to the area. So, naturally, he was always the salad guy at home until I took over. His go-to was a simple salad of arugula or radicchio tossed with a homemade dressing of red wine vinegar, garlic, salt, and olive oil. I, on the other hand, loved to throw all sorts of things into my salad. A few favorites were (and still are) sauerkraut, nuts, goat cheese, and seasonal veggies. And I love a good lemon dressing, like the Tijuana Caesar Dressing on page 111, because it can be tossed with just about anything.

Once you get the hang of making sauces and dressings at home, you won't be able to stop. Think minimal effort with tons of impactful flavors. Not only is doing it yourself a healthier way to flavor food without preservatives, it's also far less expensive than buying the packaged stuff.

I must admit, lettuce tossed with dressing is not typical of the ancestral Mexican cuisine. A Mexican salad would be more of a salsa, ceviche, or side dish, like *nopales*, cabbage, or *zapote* depending on where you are from. The Westernized salads being eaten in Mexico today all include conventional bottled dressing packed with chemicals and preservatives. Things such as ranch and Thousand Island in plastic bottles that don't even require refrigeration have become the norm. In many parts of Mexico, people opt for convenience, thinking packaged dressing will be easier and less expensive at the end of the day.

Even though salad dressings are not exactly Mexican, the ingredients chosen here are. The dressings in this book are meant to be paired with some of the Mexican-inspired veggies to give a boost of flavor while remaining nutritionally balanced.

## SOME DRESSING TIPS

TASTING: The best way to know that your dressing is perfectly balanced is to take a piece of lettuce or raw vegetable and dip it into your homemade dressing to see what, if anything, it needs. Simply dip and then adjust salt, oil, or acid to your liking.

EMULSIFICATION: Using a whisk or an immersion blender or simply shaking it in a mason jar are all ways to emulsify a dressing without having to get the large blender dirty. People always ask me why my Balsamic Vinaigrette (page 113) is so creamy. There's no cream added; it's simply well emulsified.

PREP AHEAD: One of the best ways to eat healthier throughout the week is by prepping a couple of dressings and sauces in advance. I recommend making three at the beginning of the week. You can pair them with meat, fish, and all your vegetables.

While I've included many of my tried-and-true salad recipes in this chapter, I also want to inspire you and empower you to create your own. Use the information below to help mix up your weekly salad routine.

## THE PERFECT SALAD PROPORTIONS

Once you can grasp the concept of how to have a simple salad each day and how to layer it based on your body's needs, I'll have done my job. The measurements below should serve two people as meals or four people as sides.

**LEAFY GREENS (4 CUPS)**
Red leaf lettuce, butter lettuce, arugula, kale, mustard greens, mixed greens, or Swiss chard

**HERBS (½ CUP)**
Parsley, cilantro, chives, basil, epazote, or a mix

**CRUNCH FACTOR (1 TO 2 CUPS)**
Shredded rainbow carrots, radish, fennel, broccoli, cauliflower, snap peas, jicama, cucumber, or celery

**FERMENTED ADDITION (1 TO 2 TABLESPOONS PER PERSON)**
Fermented cabbage, fennel, beets, and so on (See pages 146 to 151.)

**NUTS AND SEEDS (¼ TO ½ CUP)**
A handful of soaked and rehydrated nuts or premade Taco-Spiced Mixed Nuts (page 83)

**CHEESE—SKIP IF DAIRY-FREE (HANDFUL)**
Shaved Parmesan, crumbled feta, Cotija, or goat cheese

**SUPERFOODS (1 TO 2 TABLESPOONS)**
Soaked chia seeds, ginger, moringa powder, sprouts, roasted garlic, artichoke hearts, microgreens, mushrooms, nutritional yeast, or seaweed powders

**FATS**
Macadamia nuts, MCT oil or other oils, avocados, olives, nut butters, eggs, or hemp seeds

**DRESSINGS**
Recipes start on page 108.

# CHOPPED KALE CAESAR SALAD

¼ cup small brined capers (if using salted, soak and remove salt)

¼ cup avocado oil for frying

2 bunches (about 1 pound) lacinato kale, ribs removed and leaves torn into bite-size pieces, or ½ head of romaine, chopped (or a mix of both)

1 teaspoon red pepper flakes

¼ cup shaved Pickled Fennel (page 146, optional)

1 cup Tijuana Caesar Dressing (page 111)

¼ cup shaved Parmesan cheese

**SERVES 6 • PREPARATION TIME 20 MINUTES**

In just 1 cup of kale you will consume your daily value of vitamins C, K, and A, and about 120 mg of omega-3s—that's huge for a plant! I love raw kale, but some people aren't into it because it can be so tough and rigid if you don't know how to properly prepare it. I like to put the dressed salad in the fridge for at least 15 minutes before serving. This gives the acid in the dressing time to break down the kale. If you don't have time to let it marinate, just massage the kale using your hands until it becomes a bit wilted and then add the dressing and mix. You can add a little oil to your kale massage, but it is not mandatory.

1. Drain the capers and dry them thoroughly with a paper towel. You do not want any water on them or the moisture will spit in the hot oil when frying.

2. Heat the avocado oil in a small saucepan or cast-iron skillet over medium-high heat. When the oil is hot, add the capers, 1 to 2 tablespoons at a time, spreading them out with the spoon. Fry, swirling gently in the pan, until just golden brown, about 45 seconds for smaller capers and 1 minute for larger ones. Keep an eye on them to make sure they don't burn.

3. Using a slotted spoon, transfer the capers to a baking sheet or plate lined with paper towels to drain. Blot gently to absorb excess oil. Cool briefly before using.

4. In a large bowl, toss the kale, red pepper flakes, and the fennel (if using) with the dressing until thoroughly combined. Add the shaved Parmesan and capers and toss again before serving.

# SHREDDED CABBAGE SLAW

**DRESSING**

¾ cup full-fat Greek-style yogurt (or if dairy-free, use Homemade Mayo on page 71)

4 tablespoons olive oil

3 tablespoons rice wine vinegar or champagne vinegar

1 tablespoon apple cider vinegar

1 teaspoon ground cumin

1 jalapeño, minced

1 shallot, minced

1 cup cilantro, thinly chopped

1 teaspoon sea salt

2 cups chopped kale

2 cups shredded red cabbage

½ cup thinly sliced fennel

½ cup grated carrots

¼ cup pepitas (optional)

¼ cup thinly sliced radish (optional)

¼ cup sliced cucumber (optional)

**SERVES 6 OR AS A GARNISH FOR 12+ TACOS • PREPARATION TIME 30 MINUTES**

I love this slaw alone as a salad or served as a garnish for my Pork Carnitas Tacos (page 178) or Tinga Tomato-Chile Stewed Chicken (page 173). Dressing this slaw at least 30 minutes ahead of time breaks down the kale and cabbage, making it easier on the digestive system and a bit more flavorful.

1. To make the dressing, mix together the yogurt, olive oil, both vinegars, cumin, jalapeño, shallot, cilantro, and salt in a blender or by hand.

2. In a large bowl, mix together the kale, cabbage, fennel, carrots, and any of the optional ingredients. Toss the salad with the dressing until thoroughly mixed and then refrigerate to marinate for at least 30 minutes (the longer the better) before serving. I suggest doing this before cooking the rest of your meal, but it can even be done the day before and left overnight.

# ONE-DAY PICKLED SLAW

**SERVES 6 OR AS A GARNISH FOR 12+ TACOS • PREPARATION TIME 15 MINUTES, PLUS 12 HOURS PICKLING**

Quick pickling transforms the slaw into this tangy, crunchy side that you won't be able to put down. Plan to make this one day ahead and mix in my special pickling liquid. A quick way to prep these veggies is in the food processor.

1. To make the slaw: In a large bowl, mix together the kale, cabbage, fennel, carrots, and radish and jalapeños (if using). Transfer the mixture to mason jars and set aside.

2. To make the pickling liquid: Place the water, both vinegars, salt, oregano, and bay leaf (if using) in a large saucepan and bring just to a boil.

3. Pour the pickling liquid over the veggies in the jars and leave the mixture to cool to room temperature. Seal with a tight-fitting lid. I like to turn it upside down to get the mixture to evenly distribute. You can eat this after just 1 hour, but I prefer leaving it for at least a day to let the flavors infuse. This slaw keeps for about 2 weeks in the fridge.

**SLAW**

2 cups finely chopped kale

2 cup shredded red cabbage

½ cup thinly sliced or mandolined fennel

½ cup grated carrots

¼ cup thinly sliced radish (optional)

1–2 sliced jalapeños (optional)

**PICKLING LIQUID**

1½ cups filtered water

½ cup white wine vinegar

¼ cup apple cider vinegar

1½ teaspoons kosher salt

½ teaspoon dried Mexican oregano

1 bay leaf (optional)

# NOPALES SALAD

2 pounds nopales, thorns removed, diced into ½-inch to 1-inch cubes

2 to 3 tablespoons kosher salt

1 cup diced red onion

1 tablespoon minced jalapeño, plus more as needed

½ cup chopped cilantro

¼ cup freshly squeezed lime juice

2 tablespoons avocado oil or olive oil

½ cup fresh salty cheese (Mexican ranchero, Cotija, or feta)

Freshly ground black pepper

**SERVES 4 • PREPARATION TIME 50 MINUTES**

Nopales, with their bright-green flat paddles and fluorescent pink flowers, are native to Mexico and are also known as prickly pear cactus. They are a staple in Mexican recipes and are also used as a health remedy for disease treatment and for healing wounds, lowering blood sugar, imparting fiber, and helping to ease diabetes symptoms. I've always loved them cooked in eggs, juiced, grilled, or on top of a warm sope. Nopales are sold in Latin markets and some health food stores. The smaller ones are the most tender. Just make sure they are plump and very green. This is another recipe that was inspired by my time working at Rancho La Puerta, and it can be vegan if you omit the cheese.

Here, I give you the option to roast the nopales after brining them, which will give them a sweet and smoky flavor. You can skip the roasting step if you want.

1.  In a large bowl, mix together the diced nopales and salt and then set aside. The sliminess will come out with this raw salt method. After 30 to 45 minutes, rinse the salted nopales in cold water to remove the natural slime. Transfer to a strainer to dry.

2.  If you are roasting, preheat the oven to 350°F. Place the nopales on a baking sheet in the oven for about 1 hour, until the outsides just become golden.

3.  Place the nopales in a large bowl. Gently stir in the red onion, jalapeño, cilantro, and lime juice. Add the oil and stir until thoroughly combined. Top the salad with fresh cheese (if using) and pepper. Serve at room temperature.

NOTE If there are spines on your nopales, use a vegetable peeler to cut them off.

# ROASTED SQUASH SALAD

**SERVES 6 • PREPARATION TIME 30 MINUTES**

This recipe can be made seasonally with different varieties of squash. For winter, I suggest butternut, kabocha, delicata, or acorn; and for summer, zucchini and yellow and green squash.

1. Preheat the oven to 425°F. If you are using squash that has seeds, cut the squash in half and scrape out the seeds using a spoon. Cut the squash into uniform slices to ensure even cooking. I leave the skin on butternut and delicata, but that is up to you.

2. On a rimmed baking sheet, toss the squash with the oil and salt. Arrange the prepared squash in a single layer on the baking sheet, making sure no pieces touch. Roast in the oven until brown, crisp, and fragrant, 20 to 25 minutes. When done, you should be able to pierce the squash easily with a fork.

3. Meanwhile, arrange the greens in a big bowl or a long platter and top with the squash (warm or room temperature). Add the pepitas and cheese (if using). Drizzle the dressing over the salad. Season with salt and pepper before serving.

**NOTE** Make this a warm dish by serving with sautéed or steamed greens.

2 pounds squash (I suggest mixing a few varieties)

2 tablespoons MCT oil or avocado oil

½ teaspoon kosher salt, plus more as needed

4 cups thinly shredded kale, arugula, dandelion, frisée, or seasonal greens

¼ cup toasted pepitas

½ cup goat cheese or crumbled feta (optional)

1 to 2 cups Pepita Dressing (page 115)

Freshly ground black pepper

# HEIRLOOM TOMATO SALAD WITH HERBS AND FRESH CHEESE

**SERVES 4 TO 6 • PREPARATION TIME 20 MINUTES**

Is it just me or do heirloom tomatoes scream *summertime*?! This is one of those recipes that I encourage you to play around with. Leave it super-simple and let the tomatoes shine, or throw some capers or roasted pepitas on top. When tomatoes are fresh and in season, you can't go wrong.

1. Arrange the tomatoes on a platter and top with the pickled onions. Sprinkle with the salt and pepper. Sprinkle the cheese and herbs on top. Dress it with either just a drizzle of olive oil and vinegar or the Balsamic Vinaigrette. Serve immediately.

4 heirloom tomatoes (about 2½ pounds), sliced into rounds

½ cup pickled onions (see page 147)

1 teaspoon flaky sea salt

1 teaspoon cracked black pepper

¼ cup crumbled Cotija, ricotta, or feta cheese

Fresh herbs (cilantro, basil, or microgreens) for garnish

Olive oil and vinegar or Balsamic Vinaigrette (page 113) for drizzling

# TORIE'S CHOPPED SALAD

**SALAD**

2 cups leafy greens
(arugula, romaine, spinach,
Swiss chard, kale, or a mix),
chopped

2 pasture-raised eggs,
medium-boiled and
chopped or halved

4 ounces smoked wild
salmon, separated into
pieces (you can sub wild
canned fish; Tinga Tomato-
Chile Stewed Chicken,
page 173; or canned
sardines)

½ avocado, cubed

Handful of raw cashews,
pepitas, sunflower seeds,
or walnuts (soaked, see
Note page 67)

¼ cucumber, thinly sliced

2 radishes, chopped or
thinly sliced

2 tablespoons fermented
or pickled veggie of choice
(I recommend Pickled
Fennel, page 146)

Handful of crumbled feta or
goat cheese (optional)

**DRESSING**

½ avocado

3 tablespoons olive oil (or
for a brain boost, mix half
MCT oil)

2 tablespoons apple cider
vinegar

1 to 2 teaspoons cilantro
or parsley

½ teaspoon sea salt

**SERVES 2 • PREPARATION TIME 15 MINUTES**

A chopped salad conjures up images of bland, white-looking, thinly sliced lettuce. My chopped salad is exactly the opposite. It's crunchy, it's creamy, and it's satisfying. I make this at least a couple times a week for a quick lunch for my husband and me. (I work from home; his shop is down the street.) We'll have it after intermittent fasting from the night before, with just a high-fat drink (see pages 48 to 49) for "breakfast" in between. Breaking the fast with this salad around 1:00 p.m. keeps us satisfied until dinner around 6:30. Use my dressing recipe below or try my Creamy Detox Dressing (page 114).

1. To make the salad: In a large bowl, combine the greens, eggs, fish, and avocado with the nuts, cucumber, radishes, and fermented veggie. Add the cheese (if using) and mix together until well combined.

2. To make the dressing: Use a whisk or immersion blender to blend together the avocado, oil, vinegar, herbs, and salt until smooth and creamy.

3. Toss the salad with the dressing and serve.

**NOTE** I often assemble this salad the night before and put it in mason jars, keeping the dressing in a separate glass jar. I toss the dressing in right before we eat. The fat and protein in this salad keeps me full until dinner.

# CILANTRO YOGURT DRESSING

¾ cup full-fat Greek-style yogurt

4 tablespoons olive oil

3 tablespoons rice wine vinegar or champagne vinegar

2 tablespoons apple cider vinegar

1 teaspoon ground cumin

1 teaspoon chili powder

1 teaspoon sea salt

1 jalapeño, minced

1 shallot, minced

½ cup finely chopped cilantro

**MAKES 1 CUP • PREPARATION TIME 35 MINUTES**

It's been interesting for me as a nutritionist to watch different health trends come and go: soy milk (ew), juice cleansing, fat-free anything, whole-grain sprouted bread, and quinoa everything. Branding and labeling is huge for store-bought products, and yogurt seems to be hitting all the buzzwords these days. Most yogurt on grocery store shelves is not "healthy" nor is it an "important part of a balanced diet." That's because most store-bought yogurts are made quickly and on the cheap with thickening agents such as conventional gelatin, carrageenan, condensed milk, additives, sugars, or cornstarch. Good yogurt is made with live cultures, which create probiotic bacteria to benefit our guts and brains. Choose only organic plain yogurt, preferably 100 percent grass-fed, and the more fat the better. Greek-style yogurt (unlike most conventional options) is strained to remove extra liquid, making it thicker and creamier. This full-bodied sauce features full-fat Greek-style yogurt that makes for an excellent creamy salad dressing. It's perfect served with grilled veggies (see page 140).

1. In a blender or using a hand whisk, blend the yogurt, olive oil, both vinegars, cumin, chili powder, and salt. Stir in the jalapeño, shallot, and cilantro. (You can also thin the dressing by adding more oil and acid.) This dressing will keep in the fridge for 3 to 5 days.

# DAIRY-FREE GREEN GODDESS DRESSING

**MAKES 1½ CUPS • PREPARATION TIME 30 MINUTES**

This dressing is similar to your favorite green goddess dressing except that it's dairy-free. Herbs are so good for us, but I find through one-on-one consultations that many of my clients aren't sure how to use them. This recipe is a great idea to get tons of herbs in a tasty way. You can simply use it as a dip for your veggies, paired with meat, or thinned down to pour over your own salad (see page 97). Make this at the beginning of the week during your meal prep, and you will find yourself adding it to everything.

1. In a large bowl, combine all of the chopped herbs with the garlic, lemon juice, vinegar, and anchovy. Whisk in the mayonnaise, chile, moringa (if using), and salt. Add the oil while whisking until the dressing is smooth and emulsified. You can also make this in a blender if you want it really smooth and creamy. This dressing will keep in the fridge for 3 to 5 days.

**NOTE** You can easily make this vegan (or egg-free) by taking out the mayonnaise and adding an additional ¾ cup oil.

½ cup chopped parsley

½ cup chopped cilantro

¼ cup chopped chives

2 garlic cloves, minced

2 tablespoons freshly squeezed lemon juice

2 teaspoons apple cider vinegar

3 anchovy fillets, coarsely chopped

¾ cup mayonnaise (see page 71)

¼ serrano chile, or a pinch of red pepper flakes

1 teaspoon moringa powder or leaf (optional)

½ teaspoon sea salt

¼ cup MCT oil, olive oil, or a mix of oils

# SIMPLE DIJON DRESSING

3 tablespoons Dijon

¼ cup freshly squeezed lemon juice (optional)

¼ cup vinegar mixture (champagne, balsamic, red wine, or apple cider vinegar)

¼ teaspoon freshly ground black pepper

1 teaspoon sea salt

1 cup olive oil

1 to 2 teaspoons fresh herbs (dill, tarragon, chives, basil)

1 teaspoon red pepper flakes (optional)

1 teaspoon garlic, minced (optional)

½ teaspoon monk fruit sugar or 5 to 10 drops liquid stevia (optional)

**MAKES 1 CUP • PREPARATION TIME 35 MINUTES**

This is my go-to dressing. It's funny how everyone raves about it now that my husband has taken over the salads in our house. This dressing is one that you should be able to make all the time because the vinegars and mustard are pantry staples.

1. In a medium bowl or mason jar, whisk or shake together the mustard, lemon juice (if using), and vinegar mixture with the pepper and salt. If using a bowl with a whisk or hand blender (or even an electric blender), slowly pour in the oil while mixing to emulsify. If using a jar, simply add to the jar and shake well. Add the herbs and, if desired, the red pepper flakes, garlic, and sweetener. Blend again.

2. This dressing will keep in the fridge for 3 to 5 days.

# TIJUANA CAESAR DRESSING

**MAKES 1¾ CUPS • PREPARATION 15 MINUTES**

Did you know that the Caesar salad was invented in Tijuana, Mexico? Fun fact, right? Who doesn't love a classic Caesar salad? Most people don't know that it contains yummy nutrient-dense raw egg yolk and umami-rich, delicious anchovies. I love that this dressing is packed with immunity-boosting ingredients that taste delicious, too.

2 garlic cloves

1 pasture-raised egg yolk

6 olive oil–packed anchovy fillets

1 tablespoon lemon zest

¼ cup freshly squeezed lemon juice, plus more to taste

⅔ cup freshly grated Parmesan cheese, or 1 tablespoon nutritional yeast if dairy-free

¼ tablespoon stone-ground mustard or Dijon mustard

1½ cups olive oil

Sea salt

1 teaspoon red pepper flakes (optional)

1. In a blender, combine the garlic, egg yolk, anchovy, and lemon zest with the lemon juice, Parmesan, and mustard. Blend on low speed until the ingredients are combined. With the blender running, add ¼ cup of the olive oil at a time to create a smooth and creamy emulsion. When all the oil is incorporated, season the dressing with salt and additional lemon juice. If the dressing is too thick, add filtered water 1 tablespoon at a time until the desired consistency is reached. Stir in the red pepper flakes (if using) at the end. This dressing will keep in the fridge for 3 to 5 days.

NOTE Did you know pasture-raised eggs are generally safe to consume raw and provide amino acids and B vitamins?

# ANTI-INFLAMMATORY DRESSING

1 teaspoon turmeric powder

½ teaspoon sea salt, plus more as needed

¼ teaspoon freshly ground black pepper

¼ teaspoon finely minced garlic

2 teaspoons freshly squeezed lemon juice

2 to 3 tablespoons apple cider vinegar

¼ cup avocado oil

5 drops liquid stevia or monk fruit sugar (optional)

**MAKES 1 CUP • PREPARATION TIME 35 MINUTES**

Turmeric is being added to all kinds of things these days, and for a good reason. Turmeric contains antioxidants and anti-inflammatory components and is antiseptic. It can help with everything from headaches to cancer, circulation, pain, and more. Two easy ways to enhance bioavailability and absorption are by mixing the turmeric with a fat such as avocado oil or coconut oil as it is fat-soluble, and by adding black pepper (piperine), which improves the bioavailability by 2,000 percent.

---

1. In a glass mason jar or shaker bottle with a tight-fitting lid, combine the turmeric, salt, pepper, and garlic. Add the lemon juice, apple cider vinegar, and avocado oil. Shake well until the mixture is smooth and emulsified, seasoning with more salt. You can add liquid stevia here if you need that balance. I personally like it this way. This dressing will keep in the fridge for 3 to 5 days.

   NOTE If you prefer a thicker dressing, put all the ingredients in a blender with ½ avocado and blend well.

# BALSAMIC VINAIGRETTE

**MAKES 1½ CUPS • PREPARATION 15 MINUTES**

This dressing is just like me: an Italian-Mexican combo! I find people only use cilantro in Mexican cooking, but why not throw this medicinal superfood in wherever you can? Cilantro is a binder and a detoxifier, ridding the body of heavy metals. It's proven to have antifungal, antiseptic, and antibacterial properties. It's also packed with vitamins A, E, and K, as well as many essential minerals.

¼ cup coarsely chopped cilantro leaves

1 garlic clove, minced

¼ cup balsamic vinegar

¼ cup freshly squeezed lime juice

½ teaspoon sea salt, plus more as needed

½ cup olive oil

¼ cup MCT oil

5 drops liquid stevia or raw honey if not keto (optional)

1. In a large bowl, mix the cilantro and garlic with the vinegar, lime juice, and sea salt. Whisk just to combine. While whisking, slowly add both oils until the dressing is smooth and emulsified. Adjust the salt and sweetener to taste, if you desire. You can also put all the ingredients into a mason jar and shake vigorously, pulse it in a blender, or combine with an immersion blender to make it smooth. This dressing will keep in the fridge for 3 to 5 days.

**NOTE** If you made pickled jalapeños (see page 148), try adding them to this dressing.

# CREAMY DETOX DRESSING

1 avocado

¼ cup freshly squeezed
lemon juice

1 tablespoon grated
fresh ginger

½ teaspoon sea salt,
plus more as needed

½ cup MCT oil, cold-pressed
olive oil, or a mixture

¼ cup fresh herbs (tarragon,
chives, parsley, cilantro,
mint), coarsely chopped

Freshly ground black
pepper

**MAKES ½ CUP • PREPARATION TIME 10 MINUTES**

I like to add ginger to my foods, sip it as a tea, or add it to my water because it is just one of those healing superfoods that also happens to taste good. Ginger is a close relative to turmeric and cardamom and is mostly known for its therapeutic and anti-inflammatory properties. Most people know about ginger's gut-healing properties. From aiding in digestion to soothing nausea, it's definitely a travel must. But it is also known to help with menstrual cramps, regulating blood sugar, providing pain relief, improving cognitive function, and easing fungal and bacterial infections.

This thick and creamy detoxing dressing is packed with herbs and healthy fats to create a rich superfood dressing, and believe me, you will want to eat it with everything! The zesty spiciness from the ginger blended with healthy-fat avocado creates a unique flavor. I love it on my Whole Fish, Camp-Style (page 164), tossed on Torie's Chopped Salad (page 106), or as a dip with Mexican Crudité (page 80). I make it at least once a week, but in my house, it never lasts past the first couple of days.

1. In a blender, combine the avocado, lemon juice, ginger, and salt and blend until well mixed. Slowly add the oil through the top of the blender to emulsify. Whisk in the herbs and season with pepper and more salt. Store in a glass container in the fridge for 3 to 5 days.

# PEPITA DRESSING

**MAKES 1 CUP • PREPARATION TIME 45 MINUTES**

Pepitas (also known as pumpkin seeds) may be small, but they pack a nutrition punch of valuable nutrients. Just 2 tablespoons of pepitas contain 7 g of protein and 13 g of fiber—incredible, right? They are rich in zinc, iron, vitamin K2, copper, and phosphorus. Pepitas are one of the best natural sources of magnesium, a key mineral we are deficient in yet need for more than six hundred of the body's chemical process, like balancing blood sugar and maintaining heart and bone health. Pepitas are also rich in antioxidants (like vitamin E), which are shown to help decrease inflammation, protecting our cells from free radical damage. This amazing, nutrient-dense dressing has pureed pepitas and is one of my weekly meal planning go-tos.

1 cup soaked pepitas (see Note on page 67)

½ cup water

1 garlic clove

½ teaspoon ground cumin

½ teaspoon turmeric powder

1 teaspoon honey or monk fruit sugar, or 5 to 10 drops liquid stevia, depending on your glucose tolerance

¼ cup apple cider vinegar

1 teaspoon moringa powder (optional)

Salt and freshly ground black pepper

¼ cup olive oil

¼ cup MCT oil

1. In a blender or food processor, combine the soaked pepitas, water, and garlic with the cumin, turmeric, honey, and apple cider vinegar. Add the moringa powder (if using) and season with salt and pepper. Puree the mixture until smooth.

2. Slowly add both oils to emulsify and thicken the sauce. It may be necessary to add a little bit of water if the mixture is too thick. The dressing will keep in the fridge for up to 1 week. The dressing gets thick and separates a bit; this is normal; just bring it to room temperature and stir to restore the proper consistency.

# SOUPS & BROTHS

## SOPAS Y CALDOS

When I think of soup, I think of being cared for by my mom or abuelita. I even used to fake sickness to get soup when I was craving it (sorry, Abuela!). Just thinking about the smell of the simmering broth in the kitchen makes me feel loved and comforted. The older Mexicans in my life always had a "cure" for everything; and it never included drugs, just herbs, leaves, honey, and so forth. Even today, many locals in our pueblo still use the ancient remedies of their ancestors, and believe me, they work! I never knew that there was a scientific reason for the immune-boosting and anti-inflammatory benefits of homemade soup, with extra love, of course. Soups are easy to make, satisfying, and taste even better after a day or two. Starting with a rich broth base is the key to depth of flavor.

Soup is naturally low-carb and is a great way to get in *muchos* veggies. Most soups are not high in needed fat, though, so I will add fat through meat or toppings, like avocado, a drizzle of olive oil, or my Baja Crema with Lime (page 70). If you do not eat meat, I want to share that I have lots of formerly vegan or vegetarian clients who started their transition to meat eating with broth due to the inordinate amount of research on the benefits broth has on our body. Oh, and just so you know, each one of these clients reported more energy; better sleep; better skin, hair, and nails; and improved gut health (not exaggerating). Making your own broth will change your life, your health, and your kitchen skills. Store-bought and canned options just simply don't compare.

## NOURISHING BROTHS AND STOCKS

Making your own broths or stocks will always maximize nutrition, make you feel good, and taste way better. Homemade broth has been used for thousands of years for its healing and antiaging properties. Of course, there are now healthy versions at the health food store in the frozen section, but they are overpriced and usually stored in plastic. The hardest part about making this broth (I do it every couple of weeks) is that you have to let it simmer for at least 18 hours (on the stovetop, in the oven, in a slow cooker or Instant Pot); that's when the magic happens (after 12 hours, the gelatin releases). I recommend ordering bones online, directly from a butcher, or looking in the frozen section of your health food store. Buy a variety of bones so you have different properties such as marrow and knuckle bones. I also recommend storing tops of carrots, fennel, onions, and so forth in the freezer so you can throw these in during the last couple hours your broth is cooking for a nutritional punch. You can save veggie scraps from other recipes.

Essentially, broth is just a liquid made from the good stuff released from boiling bones. Simmering low and slow with an acid (vinegar) helps draw out the minerals, amino acids, gelatin (collagen), and vitamins from the bones, veggies, and herbs.

It takes just 5 minutes to throw these ingredients into a pot on the stove or in the slow cooker.

Sea vegetables, like kombu, dulse, kelp, nori, wakame, and arame, are great additions to your recipes. Adding kombu or wakame to your broths is a good idea if you have thyroid or mineral deficiencies or want an added mineral boost. Sea vegetables are packed with minerals and iron, which is great for balancing your hormones and for thyroid health. You can also find seaweed salts at the health food store for sprinkling on veggies.

If you aren't already making broth, let me explain why you should.

1. It tastes bomb. You can drink it alone or use it as a base for soups and braises.

2. It reduces joint pain and inflammation by utilizing glucosamine, chondroitin, hyaluronic acid, and other compounds from the broken-down cartilage.

3. It promotes healthy hair and nail growth, thanks to the gelatin in the broth.

4. It inhibits infection caused by colds and flus because of our friends the anti-inflammatory amino acids.

5. It supports our digestive systems and, more important, our gut lining.

6. It contains high amounts of calcium, magnesium, and other nutrients that play an important role in healthy bone formation.

7. Glycine in bone broth has calming effects, which may help you sleep better.

8. It helps remove toxins from the body.

9. You get a serving of protein since the bones themselves are made up of 50 percent protein.

10. This magic broth is nice on the wallet because you can use leftover bones from any meal. I usually save them up in the freezer as I cook.

## HACKS

BROWNING: Always brown your bones first. The browning process actually caramelizes the bones and adds flavor.

COOLING: The way you cool the broth affects the bacterial growth. Allow broth to cool completely on the stove or countertop before placing in the fridge.

# HEALING MEXICAN BONE BROTH

1½ to 2 pounds pasture-raised beef bones (I suggest marrow and knuckle bones, but you can also use bones from lamb, pork, chicken, or veal)

2 garlic cloves

2 onions (any kind is fine), halved

2 large carrots, halved

1 tablespoon dried oregano

1 cinnamon stick

1 orange, halved

2 tablespoons apple cider vinegar

Kosher salt

**MAKES 2 QUARTS • PREPARATION TIME 30 MINUTES, PLUS 12 TO 48 HOURS SLOW COOKING**

Bone broth heals us from the inside out. Bone broth is not just a trend, it's the ultimate superfood. Whether you are treating an ailment or just want to add some nutrient-dense flavors to your cooking, bone broth is the key. Keep it simple. Then store some in the fridge and freeze some in ice cube trays or glass containers so you always have to add to recipes (grains, soups, stews, meats, veggies, rice, on its own in a mug). If you are adding your favorite spices and herbs to this broth (and I recommend you do), throw them in at the end with salt.

1. Preheat the oven to 400°F. Roast the bones on a sheet pan for 25 to 30 minutes, until golden brown.

2. Transfer the bones to a large stockpot or slow cooker. Add the rest of the ingredients except the apple cider vinegar and salt to the pot. Fill the pot with cold filtered water until the bones are completely covered. Add the apple cider vinegar. If using a stockpot, bring to a boil and lower the heat to a simmer. If using a slow cooker, set to low and cook for at least 12 hours or preferably longer. Poultry bones can cook as long as 24 hours, and beef bones can simmer for up to 48 hours. Remove from the heat.

3. When the stock is cool enough to handle, pour through a strainer and season with salt. Once cooled, pour the stock into ice cube trays for single servings or into a larger storage container. Keep some for the week and use within 7 days if storing in the fridge. This will keep for up to 6 months in the freezer.

# CLASSIC CHICKEN STOCK

**MAKES 3 QUARTS • PREPARATION TIME 30 MINUTES, PLUS 12 TO 24 HOURS SLOW COOKING**

If you ask people the difference between stock and broth, well, you will get a ton of different answers, but I think of them as the same thing. The main lesson here is do not waste precious chicken bones! You can even throw bones in your freezer (for up to 3 months) until you accumulate a bunch to make your broth. There is nothing more comforting than the smell of simmering broth in the kitchen. That first slurp of your abuelita's chicken soup when you have a cold or just aren't feeling well really is the best cure-all. There is a reason why they call it medicine for the soul.

Once you have this base chicken stock recipe down, you can always have a batch or two in the freezer. For an easy soup, you can add lime, chiles, chayote, or whatever veggies are in the fridge. Remember, you can use a stock for cooking rice, braising meats, or just for sipping all day with lime and hot sauce. When you put stock in the fridge, the natural gelatin and collagen from the bones will create a gel that should be nice and thick. This is a good sign you used enough bones. Remember, feet have tons of collagen, so try to get all the parts to make the most diverse, nutrient-rich broth!

3 to 4 pounds bony chicken parts (such as necks, wings, backs, feet, head, plus any organs)

2 leeks, coarsely chopped

2 carrots, coarsely chopped

2 celery ribs, coarsely chopped

2 garlic cloves, unpeeled

1 medium onion, halved

2 bay leaves

2 to 3 dried chiles (such as arbol or guajillo)

1 tablespoon Mexican oregano (optional)

1 tablespoon apple cider vinegar

2 teaspoons kosher salt

4 sprigs cilantro

4 sprigs parsley

1. Place the chicken parts, leeks, carrots, celery, garlic, and onion in a large stainless-steel pot, Dutch oven, or slow cooker. Add the bay leaves, chiles, and oregano (if using). Add cold filtered water until the pot is nearly full and the bones are completely covered. (The water should cover the contents of the pot by 2 inches.) Add the apple cider vinegar and salt. Bring to a boil and then lower the heat, cover the pot, and leave to simmer. If you are not comfortable doing this on your stovetop, you can easily do this in a slow cooker. Simmer for 12 to 24 hours on low heat. Usually the stock will be reduced by a third.

2. About 10 minutes before finishing, add the cilantro and parsley to increase the minerals in the stock. Remove from the heat, strain the stock into a large bowl, and let it cool on the countertop.

3. Once it's cooled, you can put it in the fridge until the fat rises to the top. Skim and discard the fat or reserve for another use such as roasting veggies or browning meat. Store the stock in glass jars and freeze or use within 3 days if refrigerating. This will keep for up to 6 months in the freezer.

# RED BROTH POZOLE

3 cups cold filtered water

8 to 10 dried guajillo chiles

5 to 6 dried chiles de arbol (optional for a hot addition)

2 tablespoons pasture-raised lard or avocado oil for frying

3 pounds pasture-raised pork shoulder/butt (preferably bone-in but not mandatory), cut into 1-inch cubes

Sea salt or Himalayan salt

6 to 8 cups Healing Mexican Bone Broth (page 120), brought to a boil and lowered to a simmer

1 *pata* (pig foot or bone of choice, such as marrow or knuckle)

8 garlic cloves, roughly chopped

2 zucchini, cut into cubes

One 14.5-ounce can crushed tomatoes

2 bay leaves

1 tablespoon ground cumin

2 tablespoons dried oregano

1 tablespoon apple cider vinegar

1 head of cauliflower, chopped into 1-inch florets

## TOPPINGS

Shredded cabbage, assorted escabeche, chopped white onion, chopped cilantro, pepitas, sliced radish, diced avocado, lime, chicharones, fresh or dried oregano

**SERVES 8 TO 10 • PREPARATION TIME 2 HOURS**

This soup is my go-to for any winter gathering. I love the endless possibilities for toppings. Make extra and freeze it for weeknight dinners. You can use two 15-ounce cans of white hominy in place of the cauliflower if you're not strict keto.

1. Bring the filtered water to a boil. Meanwhile, remove and discard the stems and seeds from the dried chile pods. In a cast-iron skillet or heavy pan, dry-roast the chiles on medium-high heat for about 2 minutes on each side (do not let them burn). Transfer the chiles to a medium bowl and cover with the boiled water. Let the chiles soak in the hot water for 10 minutes. Transfer the chiles and 2 cups of soaking liquid to a small food processor or blender; carefully puree and set aside. Discard the remaining soaking liquid.

2. Heat the lard in a Dutch oven or large stockpot over medium-high heat. Pat dry the pork cubes with paper towels. Season generously with salt. Working in batches, brown the meat on all sides. Do not crowd the pan or stir the meat too much.

3. Once all of the meat has browned, transfer it to a plate. Add 1 cup of the broth to the pan to deglaze the bottom by scraping up any browned bits. Allow the broth to reduce slightly. If using pata, add it to the stockpot along with the browned meat. Add the garlic, zucchini, tomatoes, bay leaves, cumin, oregano, apple cider vinegar, and 2 tablespoons salt. Top with the remaining bone broth. Bring to a boil, lower the heat, and cook for 15 minutes.

4. When the soup is simmering, strain the chile sauce through a fine-mesh sieve into the simmering soup, discarding the tough bits of the puree left in the strainer. Simmer the pozole for 1½ to 2 hours. Add the cauliflower 30 minutes before serving, bring just to a boil, and lower the heat to a simmer. (If the soup is too thick, add more broth or water to the desired consistency.) The pork should be easy to shred when ready. This soup keeps well in the refrigerator for up to 3 days. Simply let the soup cool, cover it, and refrigerate.

5. Ladle the pozole from the pot into wide bowls. Serve with the toppings and let the guests garnish to their taste.

# CHICKEN TORTILLA SOUP WITH LEAFY GREENS

2 to 3 large dried pasilla or other chiles, rehydrated (see page 60), plus ¼ cup soaking liquid

2 teaspoons avocado oil or pasture-raised lard

2 chayote squash, cut into 1-inch cubes

½ white onion, roughly chopped

3 garlic cloves, peeled

½ teaspoon kosher salt, plus more as needed

1 cup fire-roasted tomatoes

1 to 3 canned chipotle chiles

8 cups Classic Chicken Stock (page 121) or Healing Mexican Bone Broth (page 120)

2 teaspoons ground cumin

2 teaspoons chili powder

2 tablespoons turmeric powder

1 large bunch greens, chopped into thin, bite-size pieces (about 4 cups)

4 small boneless, skinless chicken breasts, boiled and shredded

**TOPPINGS**

4 tortillas cut into strips and cast-iron fried or baked

Avocado, feta or Cotija cheese, cilantro, pickled red onion (see page 147), limes, Baja Crema with Lime (page 70), or goat cheese quesadillas

**SERVES 6 TO 8 • PREPARATION TIME 1 HOUR**

I enjoy soup year-round because I know how good it is for you. My friend Lorena, an acupuncturist and yoga teacher who also does wellness retreats with me, has educated me about how in her (Chinese) culture a bowl of nourishing soup for breakfast is meant to help the body balance and thrive.

I've added leafy greens to this classic soup to up the nutritional levels. While it's an untraditional twist, it adds nutrients without compromising flavor. Make extra and freeze it so you have healthy weeknight meals ready to go!

1. In a blender, combine the pasilla chiles and soaking liquid. In a medium sauté pan or in a stockpot, heat the oil over medium-low heat. Add the chayote, onion, garlic, and salt. Sauté for 6 to 8 minutes, stirring frequently, until the onion is soft and translucent. Add the mixture to the blender with the pasillas and then add the tomatoes and chipotles. Blend until smooth.

2. In a large soup or stockpot, combine the stock and chile mixture. Bring to a boil and then lower the heat to a simmer. Add the cumin, chili powder, and turmeric and simmer for 25 to 30 minutes. Season with salt if desired, and stir frequently. Add the greens and cook for 5 minutes, until cooked through. Add the chicken to warm through. Serve with the toppings.

## BAKED TORTILLA STRIPS

Cut Coconut Tortillas with Lard (page 209) into matchsticks. Preheat the oven to 425°F. Place the tortilla strips on a parchment paper–lined baking sheet. Coat lightly with oil spray or slightly coat with avocado oil. Bake for 8 to 10 minutes, until the strips are crispy. Place on a paper towel and dust them with salt.

# SOPA DE ALBONDIGAS

**SERVES 6 TO 8** • **PREPARATION TIME 1 HOUR 15 MINUTES**

This meatball soup is a very traditional recipe that reminds me of my grandma, who would always make it for us when we were sick. I love lime squeezed over a mineral-rich broth with herbed beef meatballs and some veggies. Use my low-carb rice method or, if you do not have time, soak rinsed rice in boiling water for 20 minutes. If you're not eating rice, you can use cauliflower rice for the meatballs, which is also delish!

1. To make the albondigas: In a large bowl, mix together the meat, egg, parsley, rice, garlic, pepper, cumin, oregano, chili powder, and salt. Don't be afraid to use your hands. Form the meatballs by taking a couple tablespoons of the meat mixture between your palms and rolling it into balls. If making them small, you should have around 20 meatballs. Place the meatballs on a baking sheet. Set aside.

2. Heat the avocado oil in a large stockpot. Add the onion, celery, zucchini, tomatoes, tomato paste, jalapeño (if using), apple cider vinegar, lime juice, and salt. Stir to combine and sauté on medium-low heat for 5 minutes.

3. Add the broth to the stockpot and simmer for 10 minutes. Add the meatballs to the simmering broth and bring to a boil. If the meatballs are small, they will take about 15 minutes to cook. Lower the heat, cover the pot, and simmer until the meatballs are tender, stirring occasionally, about 25 minutes total.

4. Mix the kale into the pot. Do not overcook it; just lightly cook it with the heat that's already in the broth mixture, less than 5 minutes. Season with salt and pepper. Ladle the soup into bowls and serve.

**NOTE** I often add organ meats to the meatballs to help combat my anemia. I suggest chopping up small pieces of liver, heart, and or kidneys and adding them when you can. Our bodies need these nutrients.

**ALBONDIGAS**

1 pound pasture-raised ground beef, pork, elk, or sausage

1 pasture-raised egg, well beaten

½ cup chopped parsley or cilantro

¼ cup cooked and cooled rice or cauliflower rice

2 garlic cloves, minced

¼ teaspoon freshly ground black pepper

1 teaspoon ground cumin

1 teaspoon dried oregano

1 tablespoon chili powder

1 teaspoon sea salt

1 tablespoon avocado oil

½ white onion, chopped

½ cup diced celery

1 large zucchini, diced

1 cup canned crushed or chopped tomatoes

4 tablespoons tomato paste

1 jalapeño, minced (optional)

1 teaspoon apple cider vinegar

2 tablespoons freshly squeezed lime juice

1 teaspoon sea salt, plus more as needed

6 cups broth of choice

2 cups shredded kale

Freshly ground black pepper

# SEAFOOD SOUP

**SERVES 6 TO 8 • PREPARATION TIME 45 MINUTES**

I love the combo of meaty shrimp and melt-in-your-mouth squid in this warming red tomato-chile broth. I thought this was a Mexican recipe until my dad, who grew up on the East Coast in a seafood mecca, told me it's just a simple Italian cioppino. As a little boy, he spent days clamming with his grandfather and making tomato pies at their restaurant (we now call those pizzas). Dad says to dip crusty bread in it, but I use a warm tortilla. Either way, it reminds me of the holidays with my family. You can find frozen seafood medleys (squid/calamari, scallops, and shrimp) at places such as Trader Joe's. Also, if for some reason you can't find one of these ingredients or you don't like one, just add more of the others to balance it out. Discard any shells that are open before you begin or that don't open during the cooking process.

1. In a large Dutch oven or stockpot on low heat, heat the oil and butter and sauté the garlic, fennel, onion, and salt for 3 to 5 minutes, until the mixture starts to break down and become fragrant but not browned. Add the tomatoes, tomato paste, stock, and wine. Increase the heat to bring just to a boil, then turn the heat to medium-low and simmer for about 20 minutes.

2. Add the turmeric, black pepper, chiles, and epazote to the pot and stir. Then add the fish, scallops, and squid and continue to simmer on medium-low heat for about 5 minutes. Finally, add the shrimp, clams, and mussels and simmer for another 5 minutes, until the shrimp are pink and the clams and mussels start to open. Watch closely so you do not overcook them (they will become chewy if you do). To serve, ladle the soup into bowls and top with lime juice and zest and parsley.

**NOTE** If you want to prep this beforehand, you can stop before adding the spices and the ingredients that follow. Depending on my menu, I will make this one or two nights before I plan on serving it, let it cool, and refrigerate it. I then add the remaining ingredients and continue with the recipe on the night I would like to serve it.

⅓ cup extra-virgin olive oil

4 tablespoons unsalted grass-fed butter, at room temperature

4 garlic cloves, chopped

1 fennel bulb, thinly sliced

1 white onion, finely chopped

1 to 2 teaspoons kosher salt

6 Roma tomatoes, peeled, seeded, and roughly chopped, or 1½ cups canned diced tomatoes

¼ cup tomato paste

4 cups fish stock, vegetable broth, or clam juice

½ cup dry red wine

½ teaspoon turmeric powder

½ teaspoon freshly ground black pepper

3 to 4 dried chiles de arbol, seeded and cut into pieces, or ½ teaspoon red pepper flakes (optional)

1 to 2 large sprigs epazote, 1 teaspoon Mexican oregano, or a small handful of fresh cilantro

1 pound flaky whitefish, cut into 1-inch chunks

½ pound scallops, halved or quartered

1 pound cleaned squid, sliced into ½-inch rings, tentacles halved lengthwise if large

1 pound medium tail-on shrimp, peeled and deveined

1 pound littleneck clams, cleaned and scrubbed

1 pound mussels, scrubbed and debearded

Juice from 2 limes, plus 1 tablespoon lime zest

Parsley for garnish

# HIGH-FAT SEASONAL VEGETABLE SOUP

As you will see, the two soup recipes that follow have very similar methods and can be made in less than 30 minutes. Sometimes I will add some sautéed ground meat and a handful of greens to the blended soup if I'm feeling hungry.

Remember, starchy veggies (like winter root veggies) have higher carbs and sugar, so you will want to use less of them and mix them with more fat. On the other hand, tomatoes and zucchini are watery. Remember you can always add more broth, water, or cream, but it is best to start with less liquid and add more as you go and as you taste; you can't take it away once it has been added.

## SUMMER VARIATION: TOMATO SOUP

**SERVES 6 TO 8 • PREPARATION TIME 30 TO 45 MINUTES**

5 or 6 large tomatoes, cored, seeded, and chopped (about 4 cups) with juices

2 zucchinis, sliced

3 garlic cloves

½ teaspoon anchovy paste

1 avocado

1 teaspoon kosher salt, plus more as needed

½ teaspoon freshly ground black pepper, plus more as needed

3 to 4 cups Healing Mexican Bone Broth (page 120), Classic Chicken Stock (page 121), or veggie broth, brought to a boil and lowered to simmer

1½ cups coconut cream or heavy cream

2 tablespoons olive oil

1. Preheat the oven to 400°F. In a glass casserole dish, arrange the tomatoes, zucchinis, and garlic and bake for about 30 minutes, until roasted and golden brown. If the garlic burns, throw it away as it will be bitter.

2. Transfer the tomatoes, zucchini, and garlic to a blender along with the anchovy paste and avocado. Blend until smooth. You can also use an immersion blender.

3. Put the blended mixture into a medium saucepan and add the salt, pepper, broth, and coconut cream. Simmer on low heat for 5 minutes. Stir and season with more salt and pepper, if needed, to taste. Serve in bowls with a drizzle of the olive oil on top.

# WINTER VARIATION: BUTTERNUT SQUASH SOUP

**SERVES 6 TO 8 • PREPARATION TIME 45 MINUTES TO 1 HOUR**

1. Preheat the oven to 400°F and line a baking sheet with parchment paper. Arrange the squash, parsnip, onion, and garlic on the baking sheet, and mix with the MCT oil and butter. Bake for 30 to 40 minutes, stirring halfway through, until tender and slightly golden brown around the edges. (The baking time depends on your oven. Check halfway through the roasting time. You may want to remove the onion and garlic first and allow the squash to keep baking.)

2. Transfer the roasted veggies to a large stockpot with the broth, coconut milk, ginger, nutmeg, cinnamon, turmeric, salt, and pepper. Using an immersion blender, thoroughly combine all the ingredients.

3. Bring the soup just to a boil and lower the heat to a simmer. Simmer for 20 to 25 minutes. Taste occasionally to see if you need any additional seasoning.

4. If you wish, serve with a sprinkling of pepitas, crispy bacon, and a drizzle of coconut cream. It will make you look fancy, and I love that extra crunch!

**NOTES** To cut the butternut squash, start by cutting the top and bottom off so you have a stable foundation. Use a vegetable peeler to remove the remaining skin. Cut the squash in half and scoop out the seeds (they are great roasted!). Then cut into evenly sized cubes to ensure even cooking.

1 medium butternut squash, peeled (optional), seeded, and cubed (about 2 cups)

1 parsnip, unpeeled and cubed

1 white onion, coarsely chopped

3 garlic cloves

2 tablespoons MCT oil

2 to 3 tablespoons melted butter, ghee, or coconut oil

2 to 3 cups Healing Mexican Bone Broth (page 120), Classic Chicken Stock (page 121), or veggie broth, warmed to a simmer

1½ cups coconut cream or heavy cream, plus more for drizzling

¼ cup freshly grated ginger, or 1 teaspoon ground ginger

1 tablespoon nutmeg

1 tablespoon cinnamon

2 to 3 tablespoons turmeric powder

1 tablespoon sea salt

½ teaspoon freshly ground black pepper

Pepitas for sprinkling (optional)

Cooked chopped bacon for sprinkling (optional)

# VEGETABLES

## VERDURAS

The idea that the keto diet wouldn't be filled with veggies is simply absurd. (Search online for the word *keto* and you will see what I mean.) When people ask me how I have so much energy and clear skin, and I tell them I'm on a keto diet, they'll often say, "That's just bacon, butter, and cheese, right?" Not exactly. . . .

No matter what your food philosophy might be, veggies should be a huge part of every meal. In fact, when you look at your plate, it should be mostly veggies.

Eating the rainbow is the best way to give your body what it needs. Think purple cabbage, red chiles, yellow beets, pink radishes, and, of course, all the greens you can get your hands on. Colors matter because each plant carries its own beneficial minerals, phytonutrients, and antioxidants.

The average American eats less than 1 cup of vegetables a day. *And we wonder why we're bloated and not feeling our best.* In my practice, I've been able to change the way people think about veggies. Most clients come to me eating only a few types of veggies, like carrots, cucumbers, and potatoes. They tell me they don't have a taste for much else, and I realize most people simply don't know how to properly prepare veggies.

If you've grown up with stinky boiled brussels sprouts and mushy steamed broccoli, I understand why those vegetables don't sound good to you. Veggies should be layered with texture and deep flavors and slathered in healthy fats to optimize their taste and nutrient bioavailability. Most vitamins and micronutrients in vegetables are fat soluble, meaning they need a fat to be absorbed. Eating plenty of veggies will help with weight loss, glowing skin, energy, and regularity, plus it boosts your natural immune system, preventing disease.

Personally, I like to use my veggies as vehicles for salt, spices, and fats. For instance, I roast broccoli with mustard seed powder to increase bioavailability, Himalayan salt to boost mineral intake, and grass-fed butter for extra healthy fats. Sometimes I add a squeeze of lemon for flavor, or for my friends who are just starting to like veggies or the kiddos, I'll shave some Parmesan on top. I promise that it's way better than a bag of chips.

All produce is not created equal. Due to higher-yielding crops that grow faster, look pretty, and are resistant to bugs and weather, there has been a shocking decline of nutritional density in our fruits and veggies. Our soil systems are depleted due to industrial agriculture and our toxic environment, which all contribute to the rising malnutrition (crazy, right?). Veggies must get their nutrients from the soil, but these days there aren't many nutrients left. Essentially, industrial farmers manipulate the growing environments so they don't have to grow seasonally. This is how they grow strawberries, tomatoes, and melons year-round! This is no bueno.

# HOW TO CHOOSE PRODUCE

Your best bet for getting the highest quality at the best price is buying seasonally and locally. If you can, opt for organic; it means you're avoiding toxic chemicals, herbicides, pesticides, and GMOs.

1. **HOOK UP WITH A CSA:** I recommend investing in a community-supported agriculture (CSA) box, which provides local and seasonal produce delivered to your door or picked up at your local farmers' market. A CSA is by far one of the best ways to be sure your veggies are packed fresh. You have no idea how long that broccoli at the grocery store has been sitting on the shelf. Every day it's not in the ground, it loses vitamins and minerals.

2. **SHOP YOUR LOCAL FARMERS' MARKETS:** Support your local farmers' markets! When I had my farm, I worked about eight of these in San Diego County, selling veggies and fruit directly from my farm. Don't be afraid to ask questions and build a relationship with your farmers. Even if they aren't certified organic, they may still run a farm with organic practices and just not have the money to afford certification. If you buy local and build relationships with local farmers, you don't always have to buy organic.

3. **CHECK OUT THE HEALTH FOOD STORE:** Health food stores are a great resource for clean products. But try to avoid organic produce that's shipped across long distances as they lose nutrients.

4. **SOAK YOUR VEGGIES:** Fill your sink with water and add 2 cups white vinegar. Soak your veggies for 5 to 10 minutes, carefully scrubbing any oily substances off the produce. Remember, tap water contains toxic chemicals, so using filtered water is your best option. Do this even with your organic vegetables.

5. **KNOW THE DIRTY:** Check out the Environmental Working Group's Dirty Dozen for a list of what produce has the most pesticides and what has the least (www.ewg.org).

# MEXICAN RED CAULIFLOWER RICE

½ cup canned tomatoes (any kind is fine)

2 garlic cloves, minced

¼ cup finely chopped white onion

½ teaspoon kosher salt, plus more as needed

½ teaspoon ground cumin

2 tablespoons grass-fed butter, ghee, or rendered lard

3 cups cauliflower rice

1 serrano or jalapeño chile, stems and seeds removed, minced

¼ to ½ cup Classic Chicken Stock (page 121) or Healing Mexican Bone Broth (page 120)

Juice of 2 limes

Lime wedges for serving

**SERVES 4 • PREPARATION TIME 20 MINUTES**

This is my veggie version of Mexican red rice, which is a staple in Mexico. Although this variation is not traditional, it is keto approved. I love serving this rice as part of a bowl with my Probiotic Guacamole (page 91), One-Day Pickled Slaw (page 101), and either Pork Carnitas Tacos (page 178) or Herb-Crusted Baked Fish (page 165).

There are tons of options for cauliflower rice these days. You can find it in the frozen section anywhere from Costco to Trader Joe's. You can also make your own out of whole cauliflower with a box grater or food processor. If you are using a frozen version, make sure you get the excess water out by steaming it or draining well beforehand.

1. In a blender or food processor, puree the tomatoes, garlic, onion, salt, and cumin until smooth. Set aside.

2. In a heavy pan over medium heat, melt the butter and sauté the cauliflower rice for 3 to 5 minute, until cooked through. If it is watery, steam it until the excess liquid evaporates. Add the minced chile and cook for about 2 minutes, until it has softened.

3. Pour the blended tomato mixture over the rice and stir to combine, scraping the bottom of the pan. Once the tomato mixture has been absorbed, add the broth. Turn the heat to low and cook for about 5 minutes, until the liquid has evaporated and the rice is tender.

4. Remove the rice from the heat and gently stir in the lime juice, seasoning with more salt if desired. Serve with lime wedges.

# CARAMELIZED ONIONS AND CHILES

**SERVES 2 TO 4 • PREPARATION TIME 30 MINUTES**

No, caramelized onions do not contain sugar. Every time I make them for someone, I am asked that question. In reality, it is quite the opposite; the slow cooking process breaks down the natural sugars of the onion. Caramelization is a simple process that adds richness and complexity to a dressing or to complement your protein. If you want to double the batch, just do not overcrowd the pan. You can add more once the first batch starts to soften and shrink from the cooking process. Use to top any tacos.

2 tablespoons avocado oil or olive oil

4 white or yellow onions, sliced thin

2 teaspoons sea salt

2 tablespoons grass-fed butter or ghee

4 to 6 chiles (poblano, jalapeno, serrano, Anaheim), stems and seeds removed, chopped

1. In a pan over medium-low heat, warm the oil. Add the onions and salt and cook, stirring often. After about 10 minutes, they will be translucent and soft.

2. Add the butter and chiles to the pan. Stir often, scraping the bottom of pan, and sauté for another 15 minutes. The chiles should soften. (Do not walk away in case they burn.) Store in the fridge and use within 3 days.

# CHILE GUERO IN LIME AND AMINOS

**SERVES 4 TO 6 • PREPARATION TIME 20 MINUTES, PLUS 1 DAY MARINATING**

This is a taco-shop favorite. These peppers are generally mild with an occasional hot one, similar to Padrón peppers. Marinating these overnight makes them so dang good, I could eat the whole batch.

¼ cup avocado oil

20 chiles gueros (Hungarian Wax peppers)

¼ cup freshly squeezed lime juice

½ cup coconut aminos or liquid aminos

½ cup water

1 teaspoon kosher salt

1. In a cast-iron skillet over medium heat, warm the avocado oil. In two batches using tongs, sauté 10 peppers in the skillet, turning occasionally, until the skins start to wrinkle and turn golden. Set the peppers aside in a glass casserole dish or large mixing bowl. Sprinkle with the lime juice, coconut aminos, water, and salt. Marinate the peppers at least a couple of hours or overnight. Store in the fridge for up to 1 week.

# STUFFED CRUNCHY SQUASH BLOSSOMS

12 squash blossoms

4 to 5 ounces goat cheese or queso fresco

1 tablespoon dried epazote or dried oregano

¼ teaspoon garlic powder

1 tablespoon roughly chopped basil

2 teaspoons freshly squeezed lemon juice

3 pasture-raised eggs

¼ cup gluten-free flour

½ teaspoon kosher salt, plus more as needed

½ teaspoon cracked black pepper

Pasture-raised lard or coconut oil for frying (about 1 cup)

**SERVES 6 • PREPARATION TIME 30 MINUTES**

*Flor de calabaza* are traditionally used in many Mexican dishes such as a simple quesadilla, soup, egg dishes, tacos, and of course my favorite—stuffed. Serve with Probiotic Guacamole (page 91), Habanero Pepita "Cheese" Salsa (page 67), or the Baja Crema with Lime (page 70).

Back when I ran my organic farm, I would sell blossoms directly to chefs, but I found that I would have to pick them in the dark and store them in black bags to keep them from wilting before they got to the destination. If you are using blossoms from your garden, cut them right before stuffing. If they're from a store, be aware that they're fragile and do not hold up well. Keep them in a dark place so they don't open and close.

1. Gently rinse the squash blossoms with cold water. Remove the pistil from the center of each flower and discard. Place the blossom on a paper towel to dry.

2. In a medium bowl with a fork, mix together the goat cheese, epazote, garlic powder, basil, and lemon juice until the mixture is smooth and well combined. Evenly divide the goat cheese mixture among the blossoms. Use a small spoon to carefully fill the interior of each flower. Close the petals and twist the end to seal the contents inside.

3. In a large bowl, whisk the eggs until frothy. In another bowl, mix together the flour, salt, and pepper and pour onto a flat plate. Carefully dip each stuffed blossom into the eggs and then into the flour mixture until slightly coated. Place the coated blossoms on a baking sheet or plate lined with parchment paper.

4. In a cast-iron or heavy pan, heat the lard until it is ready for frying, about 350°F. Drop the coated blossoms into the oil and allow them to cook for 2 to 3 minutes on each side, flipping once, until they reach a golden brown color. Use a slotted spatula or spoon to transfer the fried blossoms to paper towels to drain. Season with additional salt while hot and serve.

**NOTE** Epazote is hard to find in some areas. If you find fresh epazote and don't use it often, wash it, dry it with paper towels, and place it in a plastic bag to store in your freezer for future uses.

# TURMERIC-SPICED CAULIFLOWER AND BROCCOLI WITH CAPERS

**SERVES 4 TO 6 • PREPARATION TIME 30 MINUTES**

I believe most people think of mushy steamed veggies when presented with cruciferous vegetables, like cauliflower and broccoli. Roasting is an easy way to prepare delicious veggies for the week without having to do much. I love serving this dish with my Cilantro Yogurt Dressing. You can serve it more as a side dip, or spread the dressing out on the bottom of a large serving plate and stack the veggies on top. This recipe is great paired with my Whole Roasted Chicken with Lime and Butter (page 170).

1 head cauliflower, cut into florets

1 head broccoli, cut into florets

3 tablespoons slightly melted ghee or avocado oil

1 tablespoon turmeric powder

½ teaspoon kosher salt

1 teaspoon freshly ground black pepper

¼ cup capers in water, drained (rinse, if in salt)

2 tablespoons olive oil for finishing

1 teaspoon mustard seed powder (optional)

Cilantro Yogurt Dressing (page 108) for serving

1. Preheat the oven to 350°F. In a large bowl, toss the cauliflower and broccoli with the ghee, turmeric, salt, and pepper. Tip the veggies onto a baking sheet and use your hands or a wooden spoon to spread them evenly so they are not touching. Place the baking sheet on the lowest oven rack and bake 25 minutes, until golden. Remove from the oven and toss them in a bowl with the capers, olive oil, and mustard seed powder (if using). Serve with the Cilantro Yogurt Dressing.

**NOTE** Ghee is clarified butter, meaning it is heated to remove the milk solids, which allows it to have a high smoke point. This makes it essentially dairy-free with no traces of casein or lactose, unlike butter. It contains butyric acid, which is a short-chain fatty acid that nourishes the cells of the intestines, helping the digestive tract and the microbiome. It also helps your body fight inflammation.

# GRILLED SEASONAL VEGGIES

1 pound eggplant, quartered

2 bunches asparagus

2 zucchini (mix of yellow or green), halved lengthwise

1 to 2 bell peppers, halved or quartered

1 bunch green onions, white tips removed

1 to 2 white or red onions, quartered

1 head romaine lettuce or cabbage, halved

4 to 6 jalapeños, halved (optional)

¼ cup avocado oil, plus more as needed

Kosher salt and freshly ground black pepper

Green Goddess Dressing (page 109) or Balsamic Vinaigrette (page 113) for serving

**SERVES 10 • PREPARATION TIME 20 MINUTES**

This recipe screams *summer* to me. This is my go-to side dish because it complements everything from fish to meat. All you need is a grill and some veggies.

1. Light a clean grill and set it to medium heat. In a large bowl, toss the eggplant, asparagus, zucchini, bell peppers, green onions, white onions, lettuce, and jalapeño in the avocado oil and sprinkle with salt and pepper. Grill the veggies in batches for 8 to 10 minutes, using tongs to flip them. The veggies are ready when they are caramelized and starting to brown but are not burnt (you should see grill marks). Arrange the finished veggies on a large serving platter. I like to serve them at room temperature and sprinkle with more salt and pepper and a little avocado oil.

2. Once the veggies are cooled, serve with your chosen dressing.

# QUICK SAUTÉED RAINBOW CHARD

**SERVES 4 • PREPARATION TIME 10 MINUTES**

Down in San Juanico, we have a garden, and most of the plants get eaten by the bugs. The Swiss chard always thrives, however, and there is no shortage of it, which is great for us and our staff because fresh greens aren't easy to come by in the local market. This recipe is a great side dish, and I use it as a vegetarian taco option with added mushrooms and my Vegan Cashew Spread (page 72).

Swiss chard is loaded with vitamins A, C, and K and the mineral magnesium. You don't need much more than a little oil, salt, and an acid, and it is ready in a couple of minutes.

2 tablespoons Garlic Chile-Infused Everyday Oil (page 71) or MCT oil, butter, avocado oil, olive oil, or your fat of choice

½ cup minced white onion

2 large bunches rainbow Swiss chard, roughly chopped (about 10 cups), stems and leaves separated

2 tablespoons apple cider vinegar, lemon juice, or lime juice

Pinch of red pepper flakes

1 teaspoon kosher salt

1. In a sauté pan over medium heat, heat the oil and sauté the onion and chard stems for about 2 minutes, until the onion is translucent and the stems have softened slightly.

2. Add the remaining greens, the vinegar, red pepper flakes, and salt to the pan. Stir with a wooden spoon, cover, and leave to steam on medium heat for 3 to 4 minutes, until wilted. Serve immediately.

**NOTE** If you wrap the leaves up like a baby burrito (yum), it becomes easier to slice them into strips and then slice the stems into little C shapes.

# WHOLE ROASTED RADISHES

2 bunches radishes, cut lengthwise, green tops cleaned well and reserved

1 tablespoon MCT oil or avocado oil

1 teaspoon lemon or lime zest

3 tablespoons freshly squeezed lemon or lime juice

1 tablespoon olive oil

1 teaspoon kosher salt

**SERVES 6 • PREPARATION TIME 35 MINUTES**

Roasting radishes was done by accident when deciding what to do with what came in my CSA farm box one week. In a way, I was being lazy, and I just threw them in with the rest of the veggies to roast. I was so surprised with how good they were—crunchy but sweet. I decided to test them again by roasting them solo and experimenting with the green tops (yeah, those dirty-looking things). And they were delicious, too! I am a huge proponent of not wasting food. I think it's the Mexican in me or maybe the sustainability education. Either way, if they are green, they can be eaten, and I will eat them!

1. Preheat the oven to 400°F. Line a rimmed baking sheet with parchment paper or spread some additional oil on the sheet. In a medium bowl, toss the radishes with the MCT oil, lemon zest, and lemon juice until the mixture is thoroughly combined.

2. Spread the radishes on the baking sheet so they are not touching each other. Roast for 15 to 20 minutes, until they start to get golden brown around the edges.

3. While the radishes roast, roughly chop the greens. Toss them with the olive oil and the salt. Lay the greens on a serving platter or in a shallow bowl. Once the radishes are done, place them on top of the greens to soften them. Season with more salt before serving.

## PICKLED VEGGIES AND FERMENTED FOODS

Hippocrates said, "All disease begins in the gut." And he was so right. Fermented foods have been shown to help with a multitude of health issues, plus they are delicious and easy to incorporate into your diet. Fermentation expert Sandor Katz shares in his book *The Art of Fermentation*, "Captain James Cook was famously credited with conquering scurvy (vitamin C deficiency) by bringing barrels of sauerkraut with him to sea and feeding it to his crews, daily." That's pretty neat, right?

*Pickling* is a general term that refers to ways you can preserve foods using an acid, usually vinegar. But pickling does not create the beneficial probiotics and enzymatic bioactivity of fermented foods. Pickling implies preserving through acidity and often heat in a process that does not promote the growth of microorganisms.

Fermentation, or lactofermentation, is a way of pickling, but the preservation is accomplished using salt to create lactic acid (lacto), giving ferments that sour or tangy taste and smell. In the fermentation process, food is preserved by natural bacteria (*lactobacilli*) feeding on the natural sugar and starch of the vegetables or fruit, creating lactic acid, which inhibits harmful bacteria. The by-products are beneficial bacteria, enzymes, vitamins, probiotics, and omega-3 fatty acids. These bacteria enhance the health of the entire body, including aiding with digestion, improving immunity, and even reversing autoimmune disorders such as IBS and leaky gut. Without enough of these healthy bacteria in our bodies, we begin to experience symptoms such as depression, anxiety, ADHD, autism, allergies, asthma, digestive issues, skin problems, and more.

### WHY DID TRADITIONAL FERMENTATION DISAPPEAR?

Sadly, many fermented foods that would have been made at home fifty years ago are not the same when found in the grocery store. Their medicinal effects have been eradicated by pasteurization and attempts to re-create the bacteria in laboratories. When fermented foods are heated via pasteurization, the good (and bad) bacteria in our bodies are wiped out.

We can also attribute the destruction of good bacteria in our bodies to stress, poor diet, antibiotics, pesticides, and chemicals. It is crucial that we replenish our bodies with good bacteria to lead a happy and healthy life, and one of the best ways to do that is through eating fermented foods.

## FERMENTED FOODS I LOVE

**KOMBUCHA:** This is a fermented fizzy drink with a long list of flavors to choose from. You can make it at home or buy it at most health food stores. When buying, make sure your choice isn't loaded with sugar, and be sure to check the serving size (less than 3 g of sugar per serving when keto).

**SAUERKRAUT:** Sauerkraut is fermented cabbage. It's high in dietary fiber as well as A, C, K, and B vitamins. It is also a great source of iron, copper, calcium, sodium, manganese, and magnesium. This powerhouse has a variety of beneficial effects on your health and will give a boost to digestive health, aid in circulation, fight inflammation, strengthen bones, and reduce your cholesterol levels.

**MISO:** Made from fermented soybeans, miso adds a salty, umami quality to any sauce or spread. Add a tablespoon to salad dressings, hummus, stir-fries, soups, dips, or other homemade condiments. Unpasteurized (unheated) miso is best. The darker the better with miso because it is fermented longer, which also makes it saltier.

**WATER KEFIR:** Also known as tibicos, water kefir, like kombucha, is made through fermentation by a symbiotic group of bacteria and yeast. My favorite is coconut water kefir with spicy cayenne and lemon.

**KIMCHI:** This spicy Korean dish can be made from all different kinds of salted, fermented vegetables. It enhances digestion.

**COCONUT YOGURT:** A dairy-free treat that works a healthy dose of enzymes and probiotics into your daily life.

**APPLE CIDER VINEGAR:** Real, raw, unpasteurized ACV is one of my all-time favorite fermented foods. On labels, look for "unpasteurized" or "living food" with the mother. I love the Braggs or Solana Gold brands. Steer clear of anything labeled as pasteurized.

# PICKLED FENNEL

1 fennel bulb, stalks
removed, thinly sliced

1 cup distilled white vinegar

1 tablespoon apple cider
vinegar

1 cup filtered water

2 to 3 tablespoons monk
fruit sugar or xylitol

1 tablespoon kosher salt

2 garlic cloves, smashed

1 teaspoon red pepper
flakes, or 3 small dried chiles
(such as chiles de árbol), cut
into pieces

1 tablespoon lemon zest
(optional)

**MAKES 2 CUPS • PREPARATION TIME 20 MINUTES, PLUS 2 HOURS PICKLING**

Growing up, I always had *finocchio* in my lunchbox. (This is the Italian word
for fennel.) Friends would try it and make a face, and I would tell them it's
just like black licorice (anise)! Fennel is packed with fiber, and my grandpa
told me it helped with digestion. Well, I still love snacking on this, roasting it
in the oven, or throwing this pickled version on a cheese board for friends.
Pickling brings out its crunchy unique fragrance. Make sure you save the
tops in your freezer for your next round of broth (see pages 120 and 121).

1. Push the sliced fennel into a clean glass mason jar and set aside. (One
   16-ounce or two 8-ounce jars will do the trick.)

2. Meanwhile, in a small saucepan over medium-high heat, bring both
   vinegars, the water, monk fruit sugar, salt, garlic, red pepper flakes, and
   lemon zest (if using) to a boil. Remove the pan from the heat and let cool
   for a few minutes. Pour the pickling liquid over the fennel in the jars and
   let it cool to room temperature. Seal with a tight-fitting lid. I like to turn it
   upside down to get the mix to distribute evenly.

3. Pickled fennel is ready in 2 hours, but I prefer it after 1 day, when the flavors
   have infused. I like to keep mine in the fridge and eat within 1 month.

# QUICK-PICKLED HIBISCUS RED ONION

**MAKES 2 CUPS • PREPARATION TIME 10 MINUTES, PLUS 2 HOURS PICKLING**

Quick-pickling red onions is a fast and easy way to add flavor and texture to just about any dish. Besides flavor, the hot-pink color brightens up any dish you add these onions to. I always have a jar in the fridge and will often serve with salads, tacos, or alongside roasted meat. Hibiscus adds vitamin C and antioxidants, helps cleanse the blood, and aids in digestion.

1 cup distilled white vinegar

¼ cup red wine vinegar

½ cup filtered water

1 tablespoon sea salt

3 tablespoons sugar

1 tablespoon loose-leaf hibiscus (or cut open a tea bag)

2 red onions, thinly sliced

---

1. In a large pot, combine both vinegars, the water, salt, sugar, and hibiscus and bring to a rapid simmer, stirring occasionally. The sugar should dissolve and the hibiscus should seep into the mixture. Leave to simmer for 5 minutes more and then remove from the heat.

2. Meanwhile, place the sliced onions in a bowl or large jar. Pour the vinegar pickling liquid over the onions and let them marinate at room temperature for 2 hours. The pickle will last for up to 1 week in the fridge.

NOTE I will use this pickling liquid over and over again on different veggies as soon as my first batch, in this case the onions, are perfectly crunchy but well marinated. Just reheat it by bringing it to a boil and then pour it over the new batch of veggies.

# TAQUERIA-STYLE PICKLED JALAPEÑOS AND CARROTS

4 to 6 jalapeños, sliced in ¼-inch rounds (remove seeds for less heat)

2 large carrots, sliced on the diagonal in ¼-inch rounds

1 white onion, sliced thin

4 garlic cloves, peeled and smushed

2 cups filtered water

1 cup white wine vinegar

2 tablespoons apple cider vinegar

1½ teaspoons kosher salt

2 to 3 tablespoons monk fruit sugar or xylitol sugar

½ teaspoon dried Mexican oregano

1 bay leaf (optional)

**MAKES 2 CUPS • PREPARATION TIME 20 MINUTES, PLUS 2 HOURS PICKLING**

Every taco shop has this classic spicy, crunchy carrot and jalapeño dish in their salsa bar. This at-home version is something I love to have on hand for when friends come over. You can eat these all by themselves, sprinkle them on top of a taco, or serve as a condiment to your summer grilling. The rad thing about quick pickling is that you can mix and match vinegars. Try changing it up with red wine vinegar, champagne vinegar, rice wine vinegar, and white vinegar. You'll love the different flavors!

1. Place the jalapeños, carrots, onion, and garlic into two 12-ounce mason jars. In a medium saucepan over medium-high heat, bring the water, both vinegars, salt, monk fruit sugar, oregano, and bay leaf (if using) to a boil and then remove from the heat. Pour the vinegar pickle evenly over the veggies in the jars. Let the mixture cool to room temperature. Seal it with a tight-fitting lid and carefully turn it upside down to get the mixture to evenly distribute. It's ready to eat in 2 hours, but I like it the next day when the flavors have infused. The pickle will last for up to 1 month in the fridge.

# FERMENTED NOPALES

4 garlic cloves, smashed

¼ cup apple cider vinegar

1½ pounds fresh nopales, cleaned and sliced into ½-inch strips (about 1 cup)

2 tablespoons kosher salt

2 red chiles, seeded and sliced lengthwise, or 1 tablespoon red pepper flakes

**MAKES 1½ CUPS • PREPARATION 30 MINUTES, PLUS 3 TO 4 DAYS FERMENTING**

One of the things that people say about nopales (or cactus paddles) is that they are either too soft when cooked or too slimy. I find that brining them with salt beforehand cuts down on the slime factor. Nopales are packed with nutrients and are very affordable, but for some reason they are not used enough in the home kitchen. This recipe is crunchy and tangy and will go well with both breakfast and various meats.

1. Put the garlic in the vinegar and leave to marinate for 30 minutes while the nopales are being salted.

2. In a large bowl, toss the nopales with 1 tablespoon of the salt. Let rest, covered, for 1 hour. The salt should pull some of the slime out of the nopales.

3. Drain and rinse the salted nopales. Toss the nopales with the chiles and the remaining 1 tablespoon salt. Drain the garlic, discarding the vinegar, and toss the garlic with the nopales.

4. Use a muddler or blunt object to pack the nopales into a clean 12-ounce mason jar and release their natural liquid. Nopales should release enough juice to be completely submerged in their own liquid. If the nopales are not completely submerged in their own liquid, top with cold filtered water to cover. You can use a fermentation weight to hold them down.

5. Seal the jar and leave it in a cool, dry place for 3 to 4 days, checking each day. It's important to open the jar each day to prevent $CO_2$ buildup. (You can also purchase a fermentation lid online.) The ferment is ready when the brine is bubbling and has a pleasant yeasty smell. If any nopalitos float to the surface, simply discard them. Transfer to the fridge, where the flavor will continue to evolve. This ferment will last for 1 month in the fridge.

# FERMENTED CAULIFLOWER AND RADISH

**MAKES 3 CUPS • PREPARATION TIME 30 MINUTES, PLUS 3 TO 4 DAYS FERMENTING**

This recipe is a perfect example of how you can pickle or ferment pretty much anything. Cauliflower is one of the most versatile veggies and one I make in some fashion or another every week. Its unique nutrient profile, made up of carotenoids, vitamins C and K, plus some of the most important nutrients to help us fight inflammation, makes it a nutritional powerhouse.

1 head cauliflower, cut into florets

1 bunch radishes, sliced into ¼-inch rounds

1½ tablespoons kosher salt

1. In a large bowl, toss the cauliflower and sliced radishes with the salt. Use a muddler or blunt object to pack the veggies into a clean 32-ounce mason jar, as densely as possible. Top with cold filtered water to cover so that the vegetables are completely submerged. You can use a fermentation weight to hold them down.

2. Place the lid on the jar (not too tight) and leave it in a cool, dry place for 3 to 4 days, checking each day. It's important to open the jar each day to prevent $CO_2$ buildup. (You can also purchase a fermentation lid online.) The ferment is ready when the brine is bubbling and has a pleasant yeasty smell. If any vegetables float to the surface, simply discard them. Transfer to the fridge, where the flavor will continue to evolve. This ferment will last for 1 month in the fridge.

# SEAFOOD

## PESCADOS Y MARISCOS

From uni sushi dates with my grandpop to clams on the side of the road with Dad in Baja to diving for abalone in Northern California (brrr), I love seafood. I grew up fishing with my dad in front of our house in San Diego and all over Baja, which created some amazing memories and even better dinners. Ever since I was a little girl, I was taught that we eat everything we hunt or kill. Plus, we are lucky that some of our closest family friends fish for work (we had access to the literal meaning of "from boat to table" with fish freshly caught that day).

Seafood has specific types of unique fats that are extremely beneficial to our health. While there are many ways to get omega-3s from food, nothing beats seafood. Cold-water fatty fish have the highest omega-3 content in the food chain. Unfortunately, farmed fish, because of their inflammatory altered food and environment, no longer contain the omega-3s that are so beneficial to our health. They actually contain pro-inflammatory omega-6 and -9! (The same thing is happening with factory-farmed meat.)

The sad and terrifying reality is that, at this point, inflammatory fats from farmed fish are not the only issue causing seafood scares. *Bioaccumulation* describes the buildup of toxins in fish from the small plankton up to the top of the food chain. Toxins come from plastics and their by-products, industrial waste dumping, chemical-based pharmaceuticals (antibiotics, antidepressants, hormones, and so on), and pesticides and herbicides (DDT, Roundup). These toxins include arsenic, BPA, dioxins, mercury, and PCBs and affect the entire ecosystem from humans to oceans.

Farmed fish have a completely different nutrient profile. As with conventional animals, farmed fish are fed the cheapest things possible, like GMO grains, corn, and soy, which create higher levels of inflammatory omega-6 and -9. Artificial coloring is also added to make them pink or orange.

I have seen a lot of people with heavy-metal toxicity, and I believe that seafood contributes to this in part, although not as much as plastics, glyphosate, and other environmental toxins. I am not saying that I do not eat seafood. I just want to emphasize the importance of making smart choices when it comes to sourcing and being a part of the positive change to help make a difference in the ocean.

Because people are so scared of seafood now, they are generally avoiding it and not supplementing by taking a high-quality omega-3 supplement, which creates a lot of negative impacts on the body. According to a study, omega-3 deficiencies are now ranked in the top ten of American deaths. Deficiencies in essential omega-3s can cause a wide array of issues that range from things such as poor sleep and skin issues to arthritis and anxiety and can turn into heart disease and developmental issues such as dementia and ADHD.

You should eat seafood a couple times a week and choose the types of fish that are best for you and the sustainability of our oceans. Personally, I rotate wild salmon, local yellowtail, scallops, and whatever we catch ourselves or is in season. Of course, at a sushi restaurant I tend to eat whatever I am served.

I also suggest detoxing with binders (like activated charcoal and bentonite clay) after eating large quantities of seafood, for example, if you are going out to have sushi or if you eat large fish such as tuna, swordfish, or shark. I also take chlorella tablets and eat cilantro, both of which are also natural binders when eating seafood. Binders work by binding to toxins such as heavy metals, biofilms, bacteria, and candida.

## PREGNANT AND BREASTFEEDING WOMEN

The form of mercury found in fish (methylmercury) harms the nervous system and brain because it attaches to selenium in the body. Every molecule of methylmercury you consume makes one molecule of selenium unavailable to antioxidant enzymes that protect your brain against free radicals, and require selenium to function. Yet, children and adults who consume far more fish than Americans do show no signs of harm from mercury. This appears to be because almost all ocean fish contain more selenium than mercury.

Women who ate more ocean seafood during pregnancy and while breastfeeding had children with higher IQ scores and showed better overall development. Since the brain is made up of lipids and fats and you only have one chance at making the brain (and eyes) for your baby—from the beneficial fatty acids you consume; omega-3s in particular—it's important to consume essential fatty acids specifically found in seafood (shellfish and fish) and a little in plants. Remember, we cannot make these, so we have to get them through food.

There's no evidence that pregnant women or children (or anyone else) will be harmed by eating more than 12 ounces of the most commonly consumed varieties of fish. In fact, there's a lot of evidence that eating less than 12 ounces of fish a week could cause significant harm to both pregnant women and young children. Most pregnant women need to eat more fish, rather than less.

# OYSTERS AND MEXICAN CHILE MIGNONETTE

12 oysters

**MIGNONETTE**

1 jalapeño, seeds and stem removed, minced

2 to 3 tablespoons minced shallot

1 teaspoon lime zest

2 tablespoons freshly squeezed lime juice

2 tablespoons red wine vinegar

1 tablespoon MCT oil or olive oil

2 tablespoons finely chopped cilantro

1 to 2 teaspoons pink peppercorns (optional)

½ teaspoon cracked pepper (optional)

1 ounce Champagne or Cava (optional)

½ ounce Mezcal (optional)

**MAKES 12 OYSTERS, ¼ CUP MIGNONETTE • PREPARATION TIME 10 MINUTES**

Oysters contain high amounts of zinc, which helps to boost the immune system, promotes healing, and is necessary for essential growth and development. You can make the mignonette up to 3 days ahead; store in the fridge in a mason jar.

1. To shuck, or open, the oysters, use an oyster knife in one hand and a rag in the other to hold each oyster in place. Holding your oyster firmly with the flat side up and the curved side facing down, place your knife in the corner of the shell and twist the hinge part. Once it is partially open, clean the knife so no pieces get inside. Then cut the outer rim of the rest of the shell until it fully opens. Detach the oyster from the top of its shell, making sure to not spill those healthy, delicious juices. Set the oysters aside on your serving plate or store in the fridge.

2. To make the mignonette: in a medium mixing bowl, mix together the jalapeño and shallot with the lime zest, lime juice, vinegar, oil, cilantro, and other ingredients, if desired. Stir until the mixture is well combined.

3. Arrange the shucked oysters on a bed of crushed ice. If the ice is uneven, mix with a little salt water to break it down. You can top each oyster with the mignonette and serve on ice, or you can put it in a small dish in the middle and let your amigos serve themselves.(Feel free to add salt, but I left it out because most oysters are naturally salty, and the level of saltiness depends on the type you are having.)

> Try grilling your oysters! Top them with a pat of one of my compound butters (see page 73) and even a little Parmesan cheese, pop them on the grill (facing up), and cook for 3 to 5 minutes, until the butter is melted and the oyster starts to bubble. This is my summer go-to!

# GREEN CEVICHE

**SERVES 6 TO 8 • PREPARATION TIME 2 HOURS**

When we were growing up, we never added tomatoes to our ceviche like most people do, and I don't think they're needed. This Green Ceviche has a zesty, spicy edge that makes a perfect match for sweet shrimp or fish. The olive oil or MCT oil adds a creaminess that will make you want to eat the whole bowl yourself.

This can be eaten as a protein bowl, in a lettuce wrap, or with some Coconut Tortilla Chips (page 213).

It's important to choose local and sustainable shrimp. If it's being "sustainably farmed," make sure the farming environment is, in fact, using good practices. If you can find locally caught prawns, you can use them in these recipes as well. If you can't find high-quality shrimp or prawns, you can substitute halibut, rock cod, or snapper. Simply cut into ½-inch cubes and leave them to marinate with lime juice for closer to 1 hour. The fish should look white and not transparent when ready.

1 pound medium-size sustainable fresh shrimp, peeled and deveined (16 to 20 per pound) or locally caught prawns

½ tablespoon kosher salt, plus more as needed

1 cup freshly squeezed lime juice

½ red onion, diced

1 cucumber, seeds removed, diced

2 to 3 jalapeño or serrano chiles, minced

1 bunch cilantro leaves and stems, minced (about ½ cup)

1 to 2 tablespoons olive oil or MCT oil

1 avocado, cubed

1. Rinse the shrimp and cut them into ½-inch pieces or slice down to butterfly. Place the shrimp in a glass bowl. Season them with the salt and let them stand for 10 minutes. Add the lime juice and toss gently. Refrigerate, covered, for 30 minutes. The lime juice cooks the shrimp, and they will turn pinkish-red when ready.

2. Stir the red onion, cucumber, jalapeño, cilantro, and oil into the shrimp. Gently toss to combine. Season with more salt. Serve with the cubed avocado on the side or on top.

# SCALLOP AGUACHILE WITH CUCUMBER

1 pound fresh sustainably caught scallops

1 cup freshly squeezed lime juice

2 garlic cloves

1 large cucumber with skin on, sliced into thin rounds

2 to 3 fresh serrano chiles, seeds and stems removed

1 tablespoon kosher salt

¼ cup extra-virgin olive oil or avocado oil

2 tablespoons chopped cilantro

2 tablespoons reposado tequila (optional)

2 tablespoons chia gel, or 1 teaspoon moringa powder (optional)

½ red onion, sliced thin

Tostadas or Coconut Tortilla Chips (page 213), for serving

**SERVES 6 • PREPARATION TIME 1 HOUR**

*Aguachile* means "chile water" in Spanish. It is Mexico's ceviche cousin, but the scallops are lightly marinated in a puree of lime juice, garlic, chiles, and salt and then topped with fresh onion and cucumber for a perfectly balanced crunch. This is my favorite dish to make in Mexico after a long surf session. We always fight over who gets to drink the bright-green marinade at the end.

1. Pat dry the scallops and slice them into thin rounds, about 3 slices per scallop. Place the lime juice, garlic, half of the cucumber, the chiles, and salt in a blender and blend until smooth. Strain and return the strained marinade to the blender along with the oil. Blend again until smooth.

2. Toss the scallops with the cilantro and cover with the chile-lime sauce. Add the tequila and chia gel (if using) and stir in the sliced onion and remaining cucumber. Cover and refrigerate for 10 minutes. Serve with tostadas or tortilla chips.

# BAJA-STYLE FISH TACOS

**SERVES 6 TO 8 • PREPARATION TIME 30 TO 45 MINUTES**

If you have ever been down to Baja, chances are you have stuffed your face with fish tacos. While it's impossible for me to pick a favorite taco recipe, this one is a real contender. It is inspired by a taco I've been eating since I was a little girl. It comes from a taco stand on the Baja peninsula, about halfway on the eighteen-hour drive to Scorpion Bay from San Diego. The town is called Guerrero Negro, and it's known for its scallops and fish tacos—crispy on the outside and flaky on the inside. This is a keto version of that taco.

1 teaspoon kosher salt

1½ to 2 cups fine almond flour or rice flour

1 tablespoon chili powder

1 tablespoon ground cumin

2 pounds white fish (such as rockfish, halibut, cod, sea bass, or yellowtail), cut into 4- to 5-inch strips

4 egg whites, whisked

Avocado oil, lard, or coconut oil for frying (about 2 cups)

Coconut tortillas with Lard (page 209) for serving

## TOPPINGS

Quick-Pickled Hibiscus Red Onion (page 147)

Shredded Cabbage Slaw (page 100)

Probiotic Guacamole (page 91)

Baja Crema with Lime (page 70)

Salsa Bandera (page 62)

Lime wedges

1. On a plate, mix together the salt, almond flour, chili powder, and cumin. Set aside. Dry off the fish with a paper towel or dish towel. Coat the fish with the egg white mixture, then, using your hands, coat each piece of fish thoroughly in the dry mixture. Place on a plate or right in a cast-iron skillet if frying. If you are doing the baked version, arrange them on parchment paper in a platter for baking.

2. *To fry the fish:* Fill a cast-iron skillet with ½ inch of oil and heat to medium, being careful to not let it smoke (keep it under 345°F). Fry in batches; you will use less oil and will get the most consistent crispness. Fry about 2 minutes on each side, until the fish turns golden brown. (I like to spoon the oil on the parts that are not getting golden.) Make sure the fish pieces are not too close together.

   *To bake the fish:* Preheat the oven to 350°F. Bake in the oven for about 15 minutes, until the fish is golden brown on the edges. They do not need to be flipped.

3. Serve with tortillas and finish with toppings of your choice.

# WHOLE FISH, CAMP-STYLE

1 whole white fish (such as branzino, yellowtail, rock cod, sea bream, snapper, or triggerfish); (4 to 5 pounds), cleaned and scaled, cut in half and scored

4 tablespoons grass-fed butter or any compound butter (see page 73), at room temperature

Sea salt and coarse black pepper

¼ white onion, sliced in rounds

1 small orange, sliced in rounds

4 garlic cloves

2 lemons, sliced in rounds

¼ cup roughly chopped parsley, including stems

2 tablespoons olive oil

**SERVES 6 TO 8 • PREPARATION TIME 45 MINUTES**

In Baja, the season for the best seafood corresponds with the best surf: May through August. Some of my favorite memories are on the *ponga* catching dorado, grouper, yellowtail, tuna, mackerel, and bonito. The locals have a special recipe for every single fish in the water, but this one works for all of them. Cooking a whole fish can seem intimidating, especially if you rarely cook fish. I promise you, it's not hard at all, and once you present that whole fish to the table with head and tail attached, you will feel fancy. Do not be afraid to pick at the succulent meat with your fingers, being careful of the bones.

Clean your fish by taking the gills and guts out (up to you to descale or not) or have your fish-market friend do it for you. Slice four 2-inch slits on both sides of the fish along the length of the body. This helps the fish cook evenly.

1. About 20 minutes before grilling, remove the fish from the refrigerator and let it come to room temperature. Use a clean cloth or paper towel to pat the fish dry. Build a medium-hot fire in a charcoal grill or heat a gas grill to medium-high. Make sure your clean grill is oiled (I use avocado oil) to ensure the skin doesn't stick. If using an open fire (camping), get that fire going.

2. Rub the fish all over outside and inside with the butter. Liberally season inside and out with salt and pepper. Stuff the fish cavity with the onion, orange, garlic, lemon, and parsley, reserving some parsley and lemon for garnish.

3. Place the fish directly on the grill and cook, uncovered, over high heat for 8 to 10 minutes. Using tongs, flip the fish and cook for another 8 to 10 minutes. The flipping should be easy. If it sticks or resists, wait another 30 seconds and try again.

4. When cooked through, the flesh should be opaque and should easily separate from the bone with a fork or your fingers. Transfer the fish to a platter and let stand for 5 minutes. Drizzle with the olive oil and garnish with the reserved parsley and sliced lemon. Serve immediately.

**NOTE** If you do not have a grill, you can easily do this on a baking sheet in the oven. Bake the fish at 350°F for 30 to 40 minutes until the middle (thickest) part of the fish turns opaque.

# HERB-CRUSTED BAKED FISH

**SERVES 4 • PREPARATION TIME 30 MINUTES**

Even if you enjoy eating seafood when out, the average home cook or new cook is usually a bit nervous to cook seafood at home. The thing is, it's not that hard, and it shouldn't be that smelly either. If you want to dip your toe into cooking fish at home, this recipe is the perfect place to start.

1. Preheat the oven to 350°F. Place the walnuts in the food processor and pulse to coarsely chop. Add the cilantro, garlic, and oil and pulse again until the mixture is crumbly. It should stick together.

2. On a parchment–lined baking sheet or a large oven-safe dish, arrange the fish fillets skin-side down. Rub each fillet with 1 teaspoon mustard and season with salt and pepper.

3. Spoon ⅓ cup of the walnut mixture over each fillet and then gently press the mixture into the surface of the fish.

4. Bake for 15 to 20 minutes, until the fish flakes with a fork. Just before serving, sprinkle each fillet with 1 teaspoon lemon juice.

1 cup walnuts, macadamia nuts, pecans, cashews, pepitas, or Taco-Spiced Mixed Nuts (page 83)

¼ cup chopped cilantro, parsley, or dill, or a mix

2 garlic cloves

4 tablespoons olive oil

Four 6-ounce fillets of local grouper, branzino, snapper, salmon, striped bass, or halibut, ½-inch to 1-inch thick, preferably skin-on

4 teaspoons stone-ground mustard

Kosher salt and freshly ground black pepper

4 teaspoons freshly squeezed lemon juice

# CHICKEN, PORK & BEEF

## POLLO, PUERCO Y CARNE

WHOLE ROASTED CHICKEN
WITH LIME AND BUTTER 170

TINGA TOMATO-CHILE
STEWED CHICKEN 173

GRILLED FLANK STEAK
ARRACHERA 175

CAST-IRON PORK CHOP WITH
CACAO SPICED RUB 176

PORK CARNITAS TACOS 178

MEZCAL LAMB BARBACOA 179

When most people want to eat meat, they simply go to the store, buy a piece that's been cut and packaged, and take it home. There is such a disconnect between the food we put in our precious bodies and where the food came from. No one thinks (or seems to care) about what that animal's life was like, what it ate, whether or not it might have been sick or stressed or given hormones.

I subscribe to a CSA that delivers frozen high-quality meat to my door every other month. My husband and dad both hunt, so I will eat anything they kill. Unless I'm traveling or at a friend's, I have a pretty good sense of where the meat I eat is coming from. And believe me, I eat a fair amount of meat, considering I am anemic and need red meat and organ meats. The amount of meat I eat each day depends on where I am in my cycle, exercise, and goals. Every person is unique, however, and it depends on their goals, muscle mass, gender, activity level, age, and weight.

## ENVIRONMENTAL IMPACT

These days, more than ever, how you source your food matters. Making a conscious decision to spend your hard-earned dollars supporting small (and, hopefully, local), sustainable food systems has positive environmental and economic results that ripple far beyond your dinner plate.

Animals that are raised sustainably with love and respect are part of a wider food system that supports a harmonious relationship with the environment. Factory farms are growing meat simply to maximize their profits and don't care about waste, pollution, or the well-being of the animals they raise (or us). Every time you spend one dime on meat raised in these conventional systems, you are essentially casting a vote in support of giant agriculture, pollution, and greed. How you spend your money matters.

Animals that eat grass have higher levels of vitamins A and E, beta-carotene, and more of the two health-promoting fats (omega-3 fatty acids and conjugated linoleic acid, or CLA).

## PORK AND LARD

It is so important to choose pasture-raised pork and pork products. Honestly, the best option for pork doesn't fall into a neatly organized category, like beef or chicken. The best hog farmers are very small, so look for pork that is pasture-raised from a transparent source such as a farmers' market, where you can connect with the farmer. The second-best option is from a store. Look for "humane-certified," "organic," and "non-GMO," which basically mean raised with integrity.

## DECODING MEAT LABELS

Labels can be confusing. Here are the terms you need to know:

**PASTURE-RAISED:** Pasture-raised animals have outdoor access to pasture year-round, but due to weather are supplemented with organic grains.

**100% GRASS-FED:** The animal eats grass its whole life. Also known as grass-fed/grass-finished.

**GRASS-FED:** The animal was fed grass and then grain the last two to three months before slaughter to fatten them up. This is also called grain-finished.

**GLOBAL ANIMAL PARTNERSHIP (5+):** This is a nonprofit that looks at three overlapping components that contribute to good farm-animal welfare—emotional well-being, natural living, and health and productivity. They work with a scale from 1 to 5, with 5 being the highest quality. This also means there was an on-site inspection.

**CERTIFIED HUMANE:** This nonprofit certification is dedicated to improving production from birth through slaughter.

**CERTIFIED ORGANIC:** Animals are fed organic grains but don't necessarily have access to a pasture, meaning they eat organic food but may live indoors their whole lives.

**FREE-RANGE:** This is a very misleading term. There is no inspection, and it doesn't necessarily mean the animal went outside. They do have a door to go outside, but that doesn't mean they do.

**ANIMAL WELFARE APPROVED:** The label standards for this require an on-farm inspection showing that all animals must be raised on a pasture or range by independent farmers. Certified Animal Welfare Approved incorporates the most comprehensive standards for high-welfare farming.

**NATURAL:** Can still be fed GMO feed and given hormones and antibiotics. Natural has virtually no regulation.

# WHOLE ROASTED CHICKEN WITH LIME AND BUTTER

1 pasture-raised whole chicken (about 5 pounds), at room temperature

½ cup grass-fed butter or ghee

1 teaspoon garlic salt, or 1 garlic head

Generous 2 teaspoons kosher salt

Freshly ground black pepper

2 limes, halved

¾ cup Mexican Healing Bone Broth (page 120)

**MAKES 1 ROASTED CHICKEN • PREPARATION TIME 1+ HOUR**

If you eat meat, you should be able to make a roast chicken. It is a classic staple that you will make over and over again. You can save leftover meat and transform it into my Tinga Tomato-Chile Stewed Chicken (page 173), or you can add to any salad for extra protein. Even if you finish the whole bird, the bones can be used to make a beautiful soup base. See page 121 for my Classic Chicken Stock recipe.

1. Preheat the oven to 425°F. Pat the chicken dry using paper towels (unbleached, of course). Place the dried chicken, breast-side up, in a cast-iron skillet.

2. Melt the butter in a separate saucepan. With the chicken legs facing you, use a knife to cut through the skin area between the leg and breast.

3. Season the chicken with the garlic salt or garlic head. If using the garlic head, separate it into cloves and place some of the cloves inside the breast cavity and scatter the rest alongside the chicken in the skillet. Drizzle the melted butter all over the chicken. Liberally season with the salt and pepper, even inside the breast cavity and on the legs and wings. Place the limes cut-side down in the skillet around the chicken. Set the skillet with the chicken into the oven. Roast for 30 minutes and then add the broth, basting the chicken with the broth and its own juices.

4. Roast for another 30 to 35 minutes. Make sure you check the chicken when an hour has passed by removing it from the skillet (the cast iron is hot, so do not use your hands) and using a knife or fork to poke the inside of the breast (close to where you cut) to see if the juice runs clear. If it is still pink, put it back in the oven for 5 minutes. You can also insert a thermometer into the thickest part of the bird and make sure it has reached a temperature of 165°F.

5. Let the chicken rest for 15 minutes. Top with its juices, using a spoon, before serving.

# TINGA TOMATO-CHILE STEWED CHICKEN

**SERVES 6 TO 8 • PREPARATION TIME 1 HOUR**

My sisters and I had a nanny named Lupita, who was a huge part of our childhood. This recipe was her specialty for our taco nights. Tinga is traditionally eaten on tostadas, but for this recipe I decided to throw it on a roasted nopal (see page 102) instead. I also make this one ahead of time and use it on a salad or on my Cauliflower Sopes (page 63) with Shredded Cabbage Slaw (page 100) and Green Tomatillo Salsa with Cilantro and Lime (page 91).

Top with shredded lettuce, Probiotic Guacamole (page 91), Quick-Pickled Hibiscus Red Onion (page 147), crumbled cheese, and Baja Crema with Lime (page 70).

1. To make the chicken: In a stockpot over medium-high heat, combine the chicken, garlic, bay leaf, salt, chiles, and chile pequin (if using). Add cold filtered water to cover by 1 inch. Bring to a boil, lower the heat to a simmer, and skim any scum that accumulates at the top of the pot. Partially cover and cook for 15 to 20 minutes, depending on thickness of the chicken. The chicken is done when no pinkness remains and you can easily pull it apart with a fork.

2. Strain the cooked chicken, reserving the cooking liquid and rehydrated chiles. Set the chicken aside to cool slightly.

3. Place the rehydrated chiles in the blender with 2 cups of the cooking liquid.

4. Add the tomatoes, garlic, salt, chili powder, epazote, cumin, pepper, apple cider vinegar, and chipotles to the blender. Blend until smooth.

**CONTINUED**

**SHREDDED CHICKEN (*DESHEBRADA*)**

2 pounds skinless, boneless chicken breasts and thighs

2 garlic cloves

1 bay leaf

¼ teaspoon salt

2 to 3 dried chiles (any mixture of arbol, guajillo, pasilla, or, for spice, pequin)

1 tablespoon chile pequin (optional)

6 tomatoes, seeds removed, or one 15-counce can crushed tomatoes

2 garlic cloves

1 teaspoon kosher salt, plus more as needed

1 teaspoon chili powder

½ teaspoon dried epazote

¼ teaspoon ground cumin

⅛ teaspoon freshly ground black pepper

1 teaspoon apple cider vinegar

1 to 2 tablespoons chipotles in adobo sauce, or more if you like it really spicy

2 tablespoons avocado oil, pasture-raised lard, ghee, or grass-fed butter

½ white onion, sliced thin (about 1 cup)

5. Heat a large cast-iron skillet on medium-low heat. Add 1 tablespoon of the oil and the onion and sauté 4 to 5 minutes, until translucent. Add the blender mixture to the skillet and bring just to a boil. Turn the heat to low and let it simmer for 20 minutes, stirring occasionally.

6. Once the chicken is cool enough to handle, shred it using two forks or your fingers. Add the shredded chicken to the sauce and simmer for 8 to 10 minutes. Season with salt if needed.

7. If serving on nopales, preheat your cast iron or grill to medium heat. Then dry char the cleaned nopal for 3 to 4 minutes on each side or until browned. You can serve warm or at room temperature.

---

### SEEDING TOMATOES

Cut tomatoes into quarters. Using a teaspoon, hold a tomato quarter in one hand and scoop out the seeds with the other. This is how it's traditionally done in Mexico—but I also want you to do it here because tomato seeds can cause inflammatory issues.

---

# GRILLED FLANK STEAK ARRACHERA

**SERVES 6 TO 8 • PREPARATION TIME 30 MINUTES, PLUS 4 HOURS OR OVERNIGHT MARINATING**

One of the best-kept secrets of grilling meat is letting it come to room temperature before cooking it. I learned this from my dad, who owned more than a dozen steakhouses on the West Coast and knows his meat. I usually take out frozen meat in the morning and cover it on the counter so it's ready for dinner. If you have meat in the fridge, take it out for an hour before cooking. Next, salting is key because it enhances the texture (especially caramelizing fattier cuts) and gives meat that rich flavor profile. Resting the meat once cooked is important. I let the meat rest for 5 to 6 minutes, flipping halfway through. This helps to evenly distribute the juices.

I like serving this flank steak with Coconut Tortillas with Lard (page 209) as a taco, chopped like carne asada, or I'll eat it for lunch with Pickled Fennel with Lemon Zest and Red Pepper Flakes (page 146), Probiotic Guacamole (page 91), and sautéed veggies or in a butter lettuce wrap. Skirt steak also works here. I call for marinating the steak for 4 hours or overnight, but you can do it in 1 hour if you're in a rush.

6 tablespoon MCT oil or avocado oil

¼ cup freshly squeezed lime juice

½ cup freshly squeezed orange juice or kombucha (low-sugar version)

2 to 4 tablespoons chipotle hot sauce, Tabasco, or Creamy Poblano Avocado Salsa (page 65)

2 tablespoons minced garlic

1½ tablespoons kosher salt

1½ teaspoons ground cumin

1 teaspoon turmeric powder

1 tablespoon smoked paprika

1 tablespoon chili powder

1 tablespoon dried Mexican oregano or regular oregano

⅓ cup chopped cilantro

One 12-ounce bottled beer (preferably Mexican, Modelo, Pacifico, and so on (optional)

Two pounds ½-inch-thick flank or skirt steak

2 tablespoons Lime Pepita Butter (page 75)

1. In a glass or ceramic casserole dish, mix together the oil, citrus juices, hot sauce, garlic, salt, cumin, turmeric, paprika, chili powder, oregano, and cilantro. If using beer (making it not so keto), add it to the marinade. Add the steak and allow to marinate in the fridge for at least 4 hours or overnight.

2. Drain the meat and discard the marinade. Make sure it has come to room temperature. Heat a grill or cast-iron skillet to medium-high heat. For medium-rare to medium doneness, grill the steak for 3 to 4 minutes per side if less than ½ inch thick. Add 1 minute per side if more than ½ inch thick. Turn the steak at least once while grilling (more if juice starts to pool on the surface). Let the meat rest for 5 to 6 minutes before slicing. Always slice against the grain for a more tender cut. Slice the meat thin and top with a generous knob of butter before serving.

**NOTE** Make sure to not burn the meat. You'll create toxic carcinogens. Adding oregano keeps the body from absorbing the carcinogens.

# CAST-IRON PORK CHOP WITH CACAO SPICED RUB

## CACAO SPICED RUB

2 tablespoons cumin seeds, toasted and ground, or 2 tablespoons ground cumin

2 tablespoons chili powder

1 tablespoon paprika

2 teaspoons dried epazote or oregano

2 teaspoons cacao powder (no sugar)

1 teaspoon cinnamon

½ to 1 teaspoon cracked black pepper

Two 2-inch-thick bone-in pork chops (about 1¼ pounds)

Coarse sea salt

1 tablespoon pasture-raised lard or avocado oil

2 tablespoons unsalted grass-fed butter

**SERVES 4 • PREPARATION TIME 1 HOUR**

The trick to these chops is that they are salted 45 minutes before cooking and they are at room temperature before throwing them on a hot, sizzling cast-iron skillet. Small tricks can really change texture. It's the difference between having a tough piece of meat versus one that melts in your mouth with smooth but crispy fat near the bone. Serve with Quick Sautéed Rainbow Chard (page 141) or a cruciferous green such as the Turmeric-Spiced Cauliflower and Broccoli with Capers (page 134).

1. To make the rub: In a small bowl, combine the ground cumin seeds, chili powder, paprika, epazote, and cacao powder. Add the cinnamon and cracked pepper and stir until the mixture is well combined. Set aside. This rub makes leftovers so save it in a jar for your next protein.

2. Preheat the oven to 450°F. Remove the pork chops from the fridge and set on a plate. Liberally salt the meat on each side and into the fat bits. Rub the spice mixture all over the meat. Allow to sit at room temperature for 45 minutes if time allows.

3. In a large cast-iron or other ovenproof skillet over medium-high heat, warm the lard. Make sure it is hot. Place the seasoned chops in the skillet and brown just about 2 minutes on each side.

4. Using an oven mitt, transfer the skillet to the oven and roast the chop until just cooked through, about 12 minutes.

5. Remove the skillet from the oven and carefully drain any excess fat into a bowl to be discarded once cooled. Set the drained pan with the pork chops on the stovetop to rest. Evenly add the butter on top of the meat. It should melt from the heat of the pan and the chops. Baste the chops with the melted butter and juices from the chops. Leave the pork to rest for 10 minutes, flipping once. This helps to distribute the juices evenly. Cut the pork from the bones, slice, and sprinkle with sea salt. Serve immediately.

# PORK CARNITAS TACOS

**SPICE RUB**

2 tablespoons sea salt

2 teaspoons paprika

1 teaspoon ancho chile powder

2 teaspoons ground cumin

2 teaspoons garlic powder

3 pounds boneless pork butt or shoulder, cut into 2-inch cubes

Avocado oil or pasture-raised lard for frying

1 cinnamon stick

1 orange, halved

1 white onion, chopped

Corn tortillas, warmed

Lime wedges

Sliced avocado

Pickled veggies (see pages 146 to 151)

Green Tomatillo Salsa (page 63)

**SERVES 6 SERVINGS • PREPARATION TIME 30 MINUTES, PLUS 3 HOURS COOKING**

This simple *carnitas* recipe is perfect for entertaining. I love how you can serve it with different homemade toppings, like my Habanero Pepita "Cheese" Salsa (page 67) or pickled veggies. Don't be afraid of lard. Fat is good for us!

1. Preheat the oven to 350°F.

2. To make the spice rub: In a medium bowl, mix together the sea salt, paprika, ancho chile powder, cumin, and garlic powder.

3. Toss the cubed pork with the spice rub and set aside.

4. Heat a Dutch oven or any heavy, oven-proof pan over medium-high heat with just enough oil to cover the bottom. Once the oil is hot, fry the cubed pork until evenly browned on each side, working in batches so there is only one layer of meat at a time.

5. When all the meat is browned, transfer to a plate. Add 1 to 3 cups filtered water to the pan and deglaze the bottom, using a wooden spoon to break up the brown bits. Return the meat to the pan and top with enough water to nearly cover the pork. Add the cinnamon stick, orange halves, and onion. Bring to a rapid simmer, cover, and set in the oven to cook.

6. After 1 hour, stir the meat. All of the liquid should be evaporated by the second hour. The carnitas should be fork-tender in 2½ hours.

7. Transfer the cooked meat to a baking sheet. Use two forks or your hands to shred the meat into smaller pieces. Set the broiler to high and place the baking sheet on a top rack. Broil the pork for about 5 minutes, until the outside begins to get crispy. Serve family-style with warm corn tortillas, lime wedges, avocado, pickled veggies, and salsa.

# MEZCAL LAMB BARBACOA

**SERVES 6 TO 8 • PREPARATION TIME 10 HOURS TO OVERNIGHT**

Traditionally, *barbacoa* is a meat dish (usually consisting of goat, beef, or lamb) wrapped in agave leaves that, in ancient times, would have been cooked overnight in an inground fire pit. Since most of us, unfortunately, do not have a backyard dirt pit, you can also make this dish in your oven at home. The technique of braising with cumin, paprika, and cinnamon creates a taste that reminds me of Sunday adventures on our summer surf trips down through Baja. The best part about braising is that you can cook a lot of meat or a little at one time. As long as you cook it low and slow, you end up with the most tender and succulent flavorful meat that melts in your mouth and can be served in so many ways. The longer you cook it, the more tender it becomes, as long as you have some kind of liquid in your pan. There are benefits to eating spicy foods, but feel free to omit some if you cannot tolerate them. This recipe takes up to a day to make, but trust me, it's worth it.

Between the spices, the smoky mezcal, and the lamb's unique earthy and gamey flavor, this is a super-rich meal. To tone it down, I like to use Shredded Cabbage Slaw (page 100) on top for its fresh vinegar taste and crunch. Or you could serve the meat on top of Cauliflower Sopes (page 93) with pickled veggies, some fermented hot sauce, and some limes. Yum!

---

1. To make the marinade: Using a mortar and pestle, food processor, or spice grinder, grind together the peppercorns, cumin, paprika, coriander seeds, onion powder, cinnamon, oregano, and salt until they become fragrant and the oils release. Add the garlic and sliced chiles, and grind together with the spices until a chalky paste forms. Using a wooden spoon, scrape the paste into a large bowl. Add the mustard, mezcal, oil, and honey and whisk until the mixture is thoroughly combined.

2. Place the lamb on a large baking sheet or other clean surface and use your hands to rub the marinade all over the meat and into any cracks or folds it might have. You can also put the meat in the same large bowl used for mixing the marinade. (This will also save you washing more dishes.)

**CONTINUED**

**MARINADE**

2 teaspoons black peppercorns

1 tablespoon ground cumin

1 tablespoon paprika

2 teaspoons coriander seeds (preferably whole, but ground works as well)

1 tablespoon onion powder

1 teaspoon cinnamon

2 teaspoons dried oregano

2 tablespoons kosher salt

6 garlic cloves

1 tablespoon sliced fresh habanero or pequin chiles

2 tablespoons spicy or stone-ground mustard

¼ cup mezcal

2 tablespoons avocado oil or pasture-raised lard

2 tablespoons raw honey

4 pounds lamb (mix of leg, shank, and neck)

2 tablespoons avocado oil or pasture-raised lard, plus more for browning

2 large white onions, sliced thin

½ cup mezcal

You might want to wear gloves to guard your hands from the habaneros (see page 59). Transfer the lamb to the fridge to rest, uncovered, for 4 hours or overnight if possible.

3. Preheat the oven to 275°F. Let the meat come to room temperature. Heat the oil over medium-high heat in a large stockpot or Dutch oven and, working in batches, brown the marinated meat on all sides. Once the meat has browned, transfer it to a large plate or baking sheet. In the pot over medium heat, sweat the onions along with the pan drippings until they are soft and caramelized, about 10 minutes.

4. Pour the mezcal into the onion mixture and scrape any bits off the bottom of the pot using a wooden spoon—this is where the flavor is! Once you've deglazed the pot and the liquid has reduced slightly, remove the pot from the heat.

5. Return the browned lamb to the pot with the onions and mezcal. Add 2 cups water (or enough until the pot is half full). Cover and place in the oven. Roast for 4 to 5 hours, until the lamb is falling off the bone and fork-tender. Remove from the oven and rest the lamb until it is cool enough to handle.

6. Once the lamb has cooled, transfer it to a large bowl or baking pan to pull all the meat off the bones. Return the meat to the pot with the onions and braising liquid, reheat, and serve. If you want to use it later, you can also broil the meat to make it crispy, like carnitas.

NOTES Traditionally, this recipe is made with lamb neck because the tendons and cartilage not only create a richer flavor, but the extra collagen helps in preventing wrinkles and is good for hair, skin, and nails. If you can get the neck at your local butcher, try it.

You can also make this recipe in a slow cooker, leaving it on low all day until the meat falls off the bone.

# COCKTAILS & SWEETS

## CÓCTELES Y POSTRES

Alcohol is by no means healthful. Do I drink it? Yes, but in moderation. However, I do care about your beverage of choice. Even though alcohol may make you feel better at the end of your day, it ultimately has no nutritional value and hurts your ability to burn fat.

Alcohol affects our blood sugar, cravings, weight loss, anxiety, sleep, and liver. If you are drinking for social reasons, just be smart about it. Believe me, I love a good handmade cocktail and a big glass of (nontoxic) wine, but you have to drink the right stuff. I recommend toxic-free wines and clean, organic hard alcohols with bubbly water and citrus.

## TIPS FOR AVOIDING HANGOVERS

- Before you even get to a party, make sure you're hydrated. Then drink a glass of water in between each alcoholic beverage. Before you go to bed, add ½ teaspoon of Himalayan salt (electrolytes) and magnesium (see supplements on page 30) to a big glass of water, and drink it before sleep.

- Add a fat (avocado, soaked chia seeds, or MCT oil) to your cocktail. Studies have shown that the healthy fats can protect the liver against free radical damage and oxidation!

- Activated charcoal absorbs unwanted toxins in the body. It is great for aiding in most gut issues such as food poisoning, food reactions, bloating, and gas, making it great for travel. Take four capsules of activated charcoal *before drinking* if consuming wine or beer. Take them *after drinking* if consuming liquor. I recommend buying charcoal from coconuts due to the high quality of the production. It should never be taken within a couple hours of your other vitamins and any medication because you will *not* absorb them!

- Stick to one type of alcohol. If you choose mixed drinks, opt for one of the recipes that follow.

- Take the following supplements before drinking: B12, vitamin C, glutathione, N-Acetyl Cysteine (NAC), and liver-supportive herbs, like milk thistle. If using binders, just make sure they are 1½ to 2 hours away from the supplements.

- Add lemon or lime to your drink instead of sugar juice or soda. Lemon is naturally alkaline!

- Wake up and start the day with one of my high-fat drinks, preferably coffee if you can tolerate it. And then fast until lunch.

- Sweat it out with exercise or a session in the infrared sauna.

Any of the following recipes can be made with or without alcohol for an equally delicious experience. *Salud!*

# KETO SIMPLE SYRUP

**MAKES ½ CUP • PREPARATION TIME 10 MINUTES, PLUS 1 HOUR COOLING**

½ cup xylitol or monk fruit sugar

½ cup water

Simple syrup is (simply) made by boiling equal parts water and sugar to make a clear liquid used to easily sweeten things. Used mostly by bartenders for cocktails, it is in almost every drink you order at a bar. From the time I was old enough to drink, I was that annoying girl ordering the "no-sugar drink."

Once you've made the simple syrup base, you can infuse it with all sorts of fun things such as ginger, chiles, and herbs, like mint, thyme, or rosemary.

1. In a pot over medium heat, combine the sugar with the water. Bring to a simmer, stirring occasionally, until reduced and syrupy. This should take 3 to 4 minutes, and the syrup should be clear and well mixed. Let it cool down. Store the syrup in a glass bottle or jar for up to a week. It does not need to be in the fridge

NOTE To infuse the syrup with ginger: Add 2 tablespoons grated ginger to the pot when you are heating the sugar water. Strain out the ginger if you want; it's totally up to you. When using herbs, I definitely strain them out. You should use this within a day. If it crystalizes add a little hot water.

# ALOE VERA GUT-SOOTHING DIGESTIVO

½ teaspoon moringa powder

1 to 2 ounces aloe juice, store-bought whole leaf (no added sugars), or homemade (see Note)

1½ ounces green Chartreuse liqueur

3 ounces gin, vodka, or tequila

4 to 6 ounces soda water or water to top

**SERVES 2 • PREPARATION TIME 15 MINUTES**

Aloe has a special place in my heart, or should I say a special place on my face! About ten years ago, I woke up on a *bonita manana* to start prepping food for my friend's wedding party and had to turn on the stove. I got on my knees to light the pilot with my whole arm inside the oven. As it turned out, the oven had actually been mistakenly left on all night (the dial was broken), so when I lit it—*BOOM!* I was surrounded by blue and red, lost consciousness, quickly came to while rolling around on the floor screaming. My best friend who was standing just ten feet away chopping veggies grabbed me and put me in a cold shower. I was in complete shock, my eyelids, lips, cheeks, and arm were completely burned. The sound of our screaming attracted three neighbors in what felt like seconds, and in no time I was covered in aloe vera (and some other interesting vegetables and potions). That sound and smell will forever haunt me. Even now, a decade later, I find my heart racing when there's no one around and I have to light the pilot light all alone. On a positive note, aloe vera heals anything it touches, and I am virtually scar-free. Thank god for Mexican medicine. So when you drink aloe vera, you're soothing the gut lining and helping with digestion and nausea. Pair it with superfood moringa and green Chartreuse (made by monks with 130 plants) and you have yourself a green *digestivo* in a cocktail.

1. In a shaker filled with ice, combine the moringa powder, aloe juice, Chartreuse, and gin. Shake until the moringa powder has dissolved and then divide between two glasses filled with ice. Top with the soda water before serving.

**NOTES** To make aloe juice at home: Take one long aloe leaf and use a potato peeler or sharp knife to carefully cut off the thorns and most of tough edges. It is necessary to cut it all off or it will be very bitter. You will find a layer of latex between the skin and inner meat. Rinse the inner meat to remove the latex, which is both bitter and has a laxative effect. Using a blender, blend the trimmed aloe leaf until smooth and add that to your drink! If you want, you can strain it, but all the good stuff is in the skin. You can find aloe at most health food stores and also ethnic stores, but you should really have some in your garden. If you aren't growing any now, buy some and plant it immediately.

Moringa can be found at any health food store or can be purchased on Amazon.

# ACTIVATED CHARCOAL "NO-HANGOVER" DETOX DRINK

**SERVES 2 • PREPARATION TIME 15 MINUTES**

I see charcoal being used in everything from pizza crust to fancy LA smoothies because it's easy to work with, has no odor, and is a cool deep-black color. But it's not just about being cool. The real reason to use charcoal is to remove toxins from your body.

1 capsule activated charcoal

Juice from 1 lemon

2 tablespoons apple cider vinegar

2 to 3 dashes of cayenne pepper

6 ounces alkaline water (see Note)

1 ounce Keto Simple Syrup (page 185)

4 ounces tequila or vodka (optional)

1. In a shaker without ice, empty the activated charcoal from its capsule and mix together with the lemon juice, apple cider vinegar, cayenne, water, and simple syrup. Add the tequila or vodka now (if using). You can also stir without ice in a tall glass. Pour over ice or serve neat.

**NOTE** If you want your water bubbly, use Gerolsteiner, not the acidic artificially carbonated infused drinks such as La Croix and San Pellegrino. (Did I just kill your dreams?)

Activated charcoal has been used in ancient medicine for many years. Back in the day (10,000 years ago), it was used to absorb poisons and chemicals; and now it's used in hospitals for overdoses. Think about this: if you spread out four capsules of charcoal, it would be the same surface area as a football field. The porous surface has a negative electric charge that attracts positively charged unwanted toxins and gas.

Incorporating charcoal into your detoxification regimen is a game changer. It helps with toxins in food, stress, lifestyle, the environment, industrial chemicals, pesticides, additives, secondary smoke, pollutants, and heavy metals. If you are like me and like to indulge in tacos and tequila every so often, then charcoal is for you.

It is definitely one of my must-haves for your travel kit and home natural first-aid kit.

# SPICY MEZCAL MARGARITA

2 ounces mezcal, preferably organic (Del Maguey, Espadin, Union)

1 habanero or jalapeño chile, sliced, plus rounds for garnish

2 ounces tequila

1½ ounces freshly squeezed lime juice, plus lime rounds, for garnish

1 to 2 teaspoons Keto Simple Syrup (page 185)

Dash of habanero bitters

**SERVES 2 • PREPARATION TIME 15 MINUTES**

Who doesn't love a margarita, especially with tacos or on vacation on a beach somewhere? Well, most margaritas (yes, even the "skinny" ones) are packed with sugars from simple syrups and sweet and sour mix. Remember, sugar equals hangover, inflammation, and calories. I like to salt the rim because I am fancy like that. If you do not like mezcal, you can substitute another 2 ounces of tequila.

1. In a cup or bowl, infuse the mezcal with the chile for 20 minutes or longer, depending on how hot you like it.

2. In a shaker with ice, combine the tequila, infused mezcal, lime juice, simple syrup, and bitters. Shake and pour into two glasses. Garnish with lime and chile rounds.

# CUCUMBER MARGARITA

1 large cucumber, coarsely chopped, plus slices for garnish

2 teaspoons MCT oil

4 ounces tequila

3 ounces freshly squeezed lime juice, plus lime rounds, for garnish

1 to 2 teaspoons Keto Simple Syrup (page 185)

4 ounces soda water for topping

**SERVES 2 • PREPARATION TIME 15 MINUTES**

Cucumbers and tequila are my go-to refreshing combination for hot weekend days. Cucumbers are made up of 95 percent water and tons of fiber, making them hydrating and great for gut health. Add a healthy fat, like MCT oil to the drink (pictured at right) to help you feel satisfied.

1. Place the chopped cucumber and MCT oil in a blender and blend on high for 10 seconds. Pour through a strainer, separating the juice from the pulp and saving the pulp for the drink.

2. In a shaker with ice, combine the tequila, cucumber juice and pulp, lime juice, and simple syrup. Shake and strain into two glasses filled with ice. Top with soda water and garnish with sliced cucumber and lime.

# AGUA DE JAMAICA WITH MEZCAL

**SERVES 2 • PREPARATION TIME 20 MINUTES**

Agua de Jamaica, also known as hibiscus tea, is prepared by boiling parts of the hibiscus plant, which creates a deep red tart liquid that you can drink hot or cold. It has been used as a medicinal tea in Mexico to treat inflammatory conditions, UTIs, and high blood pressure, and it supports the body's oxidative stress with its naturally occurring antioxidants.

Agua de Jamaica is so delicious and is something we always have at our hotel in Baja for guests. We infuse it with cinnamon, orange, mint, or whatever other seasonal goodies we have on hand. Last summer, we opened a little restaurant and bar and I whipped these up and they were a hit all summer long!

2 hibiscus tea bags or 3 tablespoons loose-leaf hibiscus tea

1½ cups boiling water

Ice cubes

3 ounces mezcal or tequila

1½ ounces freshly squeezed lime juice

1 ounce ginger syrup (see note on page 185)

Orange wheels, for garnish

1. Brew the hibiscus tea with the boiling water, and allow it to cool. I always make extra, and I love to add orange slices and cinnamon sticks to it when I brew loose leaf tea in my saucepan.

2. Fill a glass with ice and add the mezcal, lime juice, and simple syrup. Add the brewed hibiscus tea and shake or stir well. Strain the mixture evenly into two glasses with ice and garnish with orange wheels.

## HIBISCUS RIM

¼ cup hibiscus tea leaves (loose leaf or cut from a tea bag)

¼ cup sea or Himalayan salt

1 lime, halved

To make a beautiful salted hibiscus rim, simply place the dried hibiscus and salt in a coffee grinder, or in your molcajete, and grind together. Pour the salt mixture onto a small plate. Using the lime, wet the rim of your glass, flip the glass over, and twist it into the salt mixture to evenly coat. Fill the glass with ice and pour in the drink mixture.

# AVOCADO COCONUT TORRITA

½ avocado

¼ to ½ cup fresh
mint leaves

2 tablespoons MCT oil

1 cup full-fat coconut milk

4 ounces freshly squeezed
lime juice

4 ounces tequila, preferably
organic (Espolon, Milagro,
Don Julio)

½ cup ice cubes

Couple drops of liquid stevia

Himalayan salt (optional)

Coconut Whipped Cream
(page 202) for serving

**SERVES 2 • PREPARATION TIME 15 TO 20 MINUTES**

Here in California, we are avocado obsessed. But why does it have to cost
fifteen dollars in LA for a piece of avocado toast? Here, I'm using avocado
in a cocktail, but do not let this freak you out. It's delicious! This is a perfect
keto recipe with a satisfying rich and creamy flavor.

1. In a blender, combine the avocado with the mint, MCT oil, coconut milk,
   and lime juice. Add the tequila, ice, and stevia and blend until smooth. I
   like to sprinkle a pinch of salt on top before serving. If you are feeling really
   fancy, you can serve it with a dollop of whipped cream and a sprig of mint
   on top.

Fat doesn't make you fat; sugar does. Sugar releases dopamine, making us feel really good and fueling our addiction nationwide. Studies even show that sugar is more rewarding than drugs such as cocaine. There are so many myths that come along with nutrition, and some of the biggest ones revolve around sugar consumption: *Sugar from fruit doesn't count. You need sugar for blood sugar balance. Our bodies can only use sugar as fuel. Sugar is needed for athletes. Sugar is not addictive.* Have you heard these before? Truth is, there is nothing beneficial about sugar.

For so long, people have been taught that to eat healthy is to eat less fat. As they opt for low-fat foods, they don't realize they're consuming hidden sugars (because how else would it taste good with the fat gone?). Even if there is no sugar on the ingredient label, most processed foods have it hidden under some clever name such as maltodextrin, sucralose, or sorbitol, just to name a few.

Sugar impacts just about every organ and system within the human body. Studies show that sugar is directly linked to diabetes, fatty liver disease, increased risk of cancer, imbalanced gut bacteria, obesity, asthma, poor eyesight, cognitive issues, depression, anxiety, compromised immune system, heart disease, acne, skin issues, and fertility. Plus, it ages us way faster. The Centers for Disease Control and Prevention projected a triplefold increase in the number of Americans with diabetes by 2050.

## TIPS TO KICK THAT SUGAR

- Increase healthy fats; for example, start your day with a high-fat coffee or tea (see pages 48 and 49).

- Start your day with a big glass of my Alkalizing Morning Drink (page 47).

- Practice intermittent fasting the day after your indulgence (see page 25).

- Drink plenty of water (at least half your body weight in ounces) to flush out sugar.

- Work on gut health; add fermented foods (see page 144).

- Eat more leafy greens and veggies with fiber.

- Make sure you are supporting your detox pathways—that includes going to the bathroom!

- Get sweating with hot yoga, HIIT, or an infrared sauna!

It takes ten days (or fewer) to detox from sugar, to break the addictive cycle of carb and sugar cravings that robs us of our health.

One of the quickest ways to see change in your body is by cutting out sugars. But I still indulge in healthy sweets on special occasions or during my period, so I've included some of my favorite recipes here. I use alternative sweeteners, which do not compromise your blood glucose levels. (I've checked my glucose after eating each of them because I'm that crazy.)

# HIGH-FAT SUMMER SORBET

**SERVES 2 • PREPARATION TIME 15 MINUTES**

One late summer afternoon in Scorpion Bay, a friend came to visit with a lot of mangoes. I decided to freeze some to make smoothies for our guest. I've also tried this recipe with 2 ounces of tequila to make it boozy. You can also substitute frozen berries for the mango or add coconut cream.

1 cup peeled and chopped frozen mango

2 to 3 tablespoons MCT oil or coconut oil

1 to 2 teaspoons freshly squeezed lime juice

Liquid stevia or other sweetener (optional)

2 tablespoons pasture raised collagen powder (optional)

1. In a high-powered blender, combine the frozen mango with the oil and lime juice. Pulse until the mixture starts to blend, adding water a few tablespoons at a time to thin to desired consistency. Blend in the sweetener (if using) until smooth.

2. If using collagen, set the blender to low speed and slowly blend in the collagen just to combine. You can serve right away or place in the freezer for 10 to 20 minutes, until your desired temperature is achieved.

# AZTEC ANTIAGING CHIA PUDDING

One 13.5-ounce can full-fat coconut milk or other nut milk

2 to 4 tablespoons collagen powder

6 tablespoons whole chia seeds

½ to 1 teaspoon stevia or other sweetener (optional)

1 teaspoon cinnamon

1 teaspoon pure vanilla extract

**SERVES 4 • PREPARATION TIME 10 TO 12 MINUTES, PLUS 2 HOURS CHILLING**

This pudding is one of the all-time favorites wherever I teach (for both kids and adults). It can be served at any time of the day with endless toppings (raw nuts, unsweetened coconut flakes, cacao nibs, or berries). My mom even freezes it to enjoy like a sorbet or puts it in ice-pop molds. It's best to buy whole chia seeds not the preground kind, as preground often aren't as fresh.

1. In a medium bowl, combine the coconut milk, collagen powder, chia seeds, sweetener (if using), cinnamon, and vanilla extract. Whisk until the pudding is smooth and no clumps are left. This takes a few minutes. You can also use an immersion blender, but add the collagen at the end if doing so. Cover and refrigerate it for 2 to 12 hours to thicken. Serve in small cups or bowls.

NOTE Superfood addition: Make this a chocolate-flavored version by adding cacao powder. Or try adding adaptogens such as ¼ teaspoon mushroom powder, like chaga, lion's mane, or reishi.

# COLLAGEN PANNA COTTA

**SERVES 4 TO 6 • PREPARATION TIME 10 MINUTES, PLUS 2 TO 3 HOURS CHILLING**

I used to crave something sweet after a meal, but when you're on a high-fat diet, you tend to crave sweets way less. Even though I don't crave sugar, I still love making this recipe for parties. I serve this in little shot glasses or in wine glasses for friends. The collagen is good for antiaging. Gelatin has been shown to help with digestive issues; to reverse inflammation and food allergies; soothe joint pain; boost energy; help damaged skin, hair, and nails; and so much more. I've created two versions of this recipe, one with lime and one with dark chocolate. When I am hosting a party, I usually like to make this the night before. I like to top mine with coconut shreds, lime zest, or berries.

1. In a small saucepan, mix together the gelatin and water over medium-low heat until combined. Set this aside, off the heat, for about 2 minutes to let the gelatin "bloom" and thicken.

2. *For Dark Chocolate Panna Cotta*: Add the cacao powder, cinnamon, vanilla, and cayenne (if using) to the gelatin mixture.

   *For Lime Panna Cotta*: Add the lime juice and lime zest to the gelatin mixture.

3. Add the stevia and coconut milk to the gelatin mixture and set the saucepan over medium-low heat, stirring constantly to make sure the gelatin has dissolved. Combine all the ingredients evenly; this should take only a minute or two. (I recommend tasting the mixture to adjust any of the flavors or sweetness to your taste. I like it a bit less sweet, but you can always add a couple more drops of stevia before letting it set in the fridge.)

4. Divide the mixture evenly among clean glass jars, shot glasses, or wineglasses. Cover and set them in the fridge to thicken. It takes 2 to 3 hours for the panna cotta to set. Serve chilled.

   **NOTE** If you are in a hurry, freeze for 20 minutes for a jellylike consistency.

5 teaspoons pasture-raised gelatin

¼ cup plus 2 tablespoons cold filtered water

**DARK CHOCOLATE PANNA COTTA**

2 to 3 tablespoons raw cacao powder

2 tablespoons cinnamon

2 teaspoons pure vanilla extract or powder

Cayenne pepper or ancho chile powder for a little spice (optional)

**LIME PANNA COTTA**

3 tablespoons freshly squeezed lime juice

1 teaspoon lime zest

15 to 20 drops liquid stevia, or 1 tablespoon monk fruit sugar

2 cups canned coconut cream

# DARK CHOCOLATE COLLAGEN FAT BALLS

**MAKES 10 TO 12 BALLS • PREPARATION TIME 1 HOUR 20 MINUTES**

Most fat balls you see for sale are packed with sugar and are not so focused on fat. I love my version because they are an easy way to get in your healthy fats without having to scoop oil in your mouth.

This no-bake treat is something I always keep in the freezer to curb that (now far-less noisy) sweet tooth. For this recipe, I created rich fat balls and covered them in chocolate for a satisfying and decadent dessert. You can dip or drizzle the chocolate.

If you're making these for kids, dates are a better sweetener substitution than the stevia. You can sub three to four dates (remove the pits, and soak the dates for 20 minutes in hot water to soften). If you don't soak them beforehand, add a couple of tablespoons of water. Keep in mind that the addition of dates no longer makes this recipe strict keto.

1. To make the balls: In a food processor or high-powered blender and working in two batches, combine the stevia, coconut butter, coconut oil, and vanilla extract. Blend into a paste, scraping down the sides as needed.

2. Add the coconut flour, cinnamon, almond butter, salt, cayenne, and collagen (if using) to the processor. Add the cacao nibs (if using) and pulse just until well mixed. The texture should feel a little wetter than a cookie dough. Do not overblend. Place the mixture in the fridge for about 10 minutes so that it is less messy when you make the balls.

3. Line a large baking sheet or platter with parchment paper. Take the batter out of the fridge. Use a tablespoon to scoop batter into your hand and roll into small balls. To make dipping easier, keep the balls cold until you are ready to dip.

4. To make the dark chocolate dip: In a small saucepan, melt the chocolate, coconut oil, and stevia. Stir until it turns into a thick liquid. Do not let it burn.

5. Working one at a time, use two spoons to dip the balls into the chocolate mixture, making sure they are evenly coated. After dipping in chocolate, place each ball on the baking sheet and finish with your topping of choice (mine is a sprinkle of salt). Place the baking sheet in the refrigerator for 10 minutes until the chocolate hardens. Store in a container in the refrigerator for 2 weeks or in the freezer (I like them frozen) for 2 months.

## BALLS

15 to 20 drops liquid stevia, or 1 tablespoon monk fruit sugar

½ cup melted coconut butter

⅓ cup melted coconut oil

1 teaspoon pure vanilla extract

1 cup coconut flour

1 teaspoon cinnamon

½ cup creamy almond butter or other nut or seed butter (sunflower, tahini, or cashew)

Pinch of kosher salt

½ to 1 teaspoon cayenne pepper

4 tablespoons pasture-raised collagen (optional)

Handful of cacao nibs (optional)

## DARK CHOCOLATE DIP

One 8- to 10-ounce 80% or higher chocolate bar, 1 cup sugar-free dark chocolate chips, or 3 to 4 tablespoons cacao powder

1 tablespoon coconut oil

Liquid stevia or monk fruit powder

## TOPPINGS

Coarse salt, chopped nuts, shredded coconut, cayenne pepper, cacao powder

# CACAO AVOCADO MOUSSE

2 avocados

¼ cup raw cacao powder

½ cup canned full-fat coconut milk (use the solid part if available, for extra creaminess)

½ to 1 tablespoon liquid stevia, or 1 to 2 teaspoons raw honey

½ teaspoon pure vanilla extract

¼ teaspoon Ceylon cinnamon

Pinch of sea salt

½ teaspoon cayenne pepper plus ¼ teaspoon ancho chile powder (optional)

1 tablespoon MCT oil or coconut oil

**SERVES 4 • PREPARATION TIME 30 MINUTES**

In my healthy-fats class at Rancho La Puerta, we talk about good fats, bad fats, and common misconceptions and then I make this recipe for the guests to try. It's always a huge hit! This is the simplest way to get your sweet-tooth fix. I also love making this for the kiddos because you can sneak in all types of superfoods—but leave out the cayenne.

You can top this with some cacao nibs, ancho chile powder, nuts, shredded coconut, or Coconut Whipped Cream (page 202).

1. Remove the stone from the avocados, place the flesh in a blender or food processor, and blend until smooth. Add the cacao powder, coconut milk, stevia, vanilla, cinnamon, and salt. Add the cayenne–chile powder (if using) and blend until the mixture is smooth and the ingredients are thoroughly combined. Slowly add the oil to emulsify.

2. Transfer the mixture to four ramekins or glass containers and set in the fridge to chill for 20 minutes to get a good consistency before serving.

NOTE You can also add chia seed, nuts, green powders, bee pollen, hemp seeds, or coco shreds as toppings for a superfood boost!

# COCONUT WHIPPED CREAM

One 13.5-ounce can full-fat coconut cream or coconut milk, chilled in the fridge overnight or up to 3 days

1 teaspoon pure vanilla bean paste or extract

½ teaspoon cinnamon

2 to 4 tablespoons liquid stevia, monk fruit sugar, or xylitol (blended into powder if granular sugar)

1 teaspoon MCT oil or coconut oil (optional)

**MAKES 1½ CUPS • PREPARATION TIME 10 MINUTES**

This is a nutrient-dense alternative to traditional whipped cream, which is typically loaded with chemicals, hormones, and tons of refined sugar. This version has no sugar and is full of healthy fats. Coconut cream must be refrigerated for at least one night to separate the "cream" from the liquid "milk" because it does not have any additives or thickeners. Not all brands of coconut milk or cream are equal. Look at the ingredients and make sure that there are no additives (like guar gum) that would keep the cream and liquid from separating.

I doubt you'll have any leftovers, but I love this with fresh berries or on top of my Cacao Avocado Mousse (page 200).

1. Chill a mixing bowl and mixer beaters in the fridge for 5 to 10 minutes. Scoop the solid coconut cream from the top of the can and place it in the cold bowl. Pour the liquid into a different container and store in the fridge or freezer for another use.

2. Add the vanilla, cinnamon, stevia, and oil (if using) to the bowl and whip on high speed until soft peaks form, about 2 minutes. The whipped cream will last in the fridge for 2 days.

NOTE Freeze leftover coconut milk liquid in ice cube trays and blend into smoothies to thicken.

# SPICY CHOCOLATE CAKE WITH KETO FROSTING

**SERVES 10 TO 12 • PREPARATION TIME 1½ HOURS**

Low-carb baking options are really difficult to develop (especially considering a normal cake with white flour contains about 100 grams of carbs). This recipe was inspired by one of my favorite cookbooks, *Hartwood in Tulum*. This chocolate cake is really tasty, but it's not the "cake" you know so well. Due to the different composition of all-purpose flour and low-carb flour, you need to use a couple types of flour. I provided a recipe for making your own confectioners' sugar, or you can buy monk fruit confectioners' sugar in most health food stores and online. Chile powders combined with cayenne, cinnamon, and allspice create a spicy kick that pairs perfectly with the rich cacao in this cake.

1. To make the cake: Preheat the oven to 350°F. Lay parchment paper in a 9 by 11-inch glass casserole dish or standard 9-inch round cake pan and grease with butter. Set aside.

2. In a medium bowl, with a whisk, cream the butter and sugar together. Add the eggs one at a time until each is mixed in. Gradually beat in the coconut milk and vanilla extract until thoroughly combined.

3. In a separate bowl, whisk together the almond flour, coconut flour, cacao powder, baking powder, baking soda, sea salt, coffee, cinnamon, allspice, both chile powders, and cayenne. Fold the dry mixture into the wet mixture and mix until smooth.

4. Pour the batter into the prepared cake pan and bake until a toothpick or tester inserted into the center comes out clean, 50 to 60 minutes depending on your oven. Let cool about 10 minutes, then run a knife or an offset spatula around the outside of the cake before you take it out of the dish. You can now pull out the parchment paper and let the cake cool completely.

**CONTINUED**

## CAKE

8 tablespoons grass-fed butter, or ½ cup coconut oil, melted, plus more for greasing

1½ cups xylitol sugar or monk fruit sugar

4 pasture-raised eggs, at room temperature

1¼ cups coconut milk, almond milk, or whole milk

2 teaspoons pure vanilla extract

2 cups almond flour

¼ cup coconut flour

½ cup unsweetened raw cacao powder, sifted

2 teaspoons baking powder

½ teaspoon baking soda

1½ teaspoons sea salt

2 tablespoons finely ground coffee

1 tablespoon cinnamon

½ teaspoon ground allspice

½ teaspoon ancho chile powder

½ teaspoon chipotle chile powder

½ teaspoon cayenne pepper

**FROSTING**

¾ cup unsalted grass-fed butter, cubed and at room temperature

1 avocado, pitted and mashed

6 ounces unsweetened chocolate, melted, or ⅔ cup unsweetened cacao

1 teaspoon liquid stevia, raw honey, or monk fruit sugar

2 teaspoons pure vanilla extract

1 cup keto confectioners' sugar (see below), or 8 to 10 tablespoons xylitol sugar

Pinch of kosher salt

5. To make the frosting: In a stand mixer with a whisk or paddle attachment, or using a hand blender, cream the butter on medium speed for about 4 minutes, until fluffy. Slowly add the avocado until well mixed. Add the melted chocolate and stevia. Mix until well combined. Blend in the vanilla, confectioners' sugar, and salt until smooth.

6. Frost the cooled cake. The cake will last in the fridge for 3 days.

## MAKE YOUR OWN KETO CONFECTIONERS' SUGAR

**MAKES 1 CUP • PREPARATION TIME 10 MINUTES**

1 cup monk fruit sugar or xylitol sugar

2 teaspoons non-GMO arrowroot or cornstarch (optional)

In a high speed blender, blend the sugar and arrowroot (if using) for about 30 seconds, and—*boom*—you have "powdered sugar"!

# NOT SO KETO

## NO ES KETO

Since this book is focused on keto recipes, I had to make a chapter that features some of my favorite recipes that are, well, not so keto. This chapter is still filled with anti-inflammatory, gluten-free, low-carb, healthy recipes that are oh-so-delicious. Unless suffering from a serious illness, most people can eat these dishes and be just fine. As you read in my ketosis section (see page 16), studies show that going in and out of ketosis is beneficial for most people. Eating what follows may take you out of ketosis depending on how much you eat, what exactly you eat, or if you fast. A Mexican cookbook without some recipes for beans, chips, corn tortillas, cheesy quesadillas, and a vegan tostada would not be complete, and I'd risk offending some of my family members. Eat in moderation and enjoy.

# COCONUT TORTILLAS WITH LARD

**MAKES 10 TORTILLAS • PREPARATION TIME 30 MINUTES**

Made with cassava and coconut flours, these tortillas are gluten-, grain-, and nut-free. They're high in fiber and still have that high-carb chewy texture. In developing this recipe, I wanted to create something that was grain- and gluten-free but also delicious. They may not be 100 percent keto, but they're far better than a corn or regular flour tortilla.

If you don't have a tortilla press, you can roll these out with a rolling pin, but it takes longer and is a little more difficult. Once you taste these, you'll agree that investing in a tortilla press is totally worth it!

Cassava, also known as yuca, is not to be confused with tapioca. (Tapioca is extracted from cassava and does not work the same in the recipes.) Cassava is a root vegetable, which naturally has a low glycemic index, and contains resistant starch that is beneficial because it feeds good gut bacteria in the colon. Cassava also contains saponins, which are naturally occurring phytochemicals that help lower blood sugar, bind and remove bile, and remove toxins.

Most Mexicans use a leftover plastic bag cut out into rounds for pressing the tortillas. Yes, like the ones you get from the store. I am trying to have a plastic-free book, so just pretend I never told you that. Parchment paper or waxed paper also works, and that's what I've called for.

1 cup cassava flour, plus more as needed

2 tablespoons coconut flour

½ teaspoon apple cider vinegar

¼ teaspoon kosher salt

¼ cup pasture-raised lard, ghee, or coconut oil

1 cup warm water, or more for desired consistency

1. In a large bowl, whisk together the cassava flour, coconut flour, vinegar, and salt. Add the lard and mix. Slowly add the warm water and mix with your hands until the dough forms a soft consistency. If it's too dry, add more water 1 tablespoon at a time; if it is too wet, add a little more cassava flour. I keep my hands slightly wet while working the dough.

2. Heat a cast-iron skillet or *comal* to medium-high heat. On a floured work surface, roll the dough evenly into ten balls. For each dough ball, cut out two squares of parchment paper or waxed paper that match the size of the tortilla press. This paper will act as a barrier between the dough and the tortilla press.

**CONTINUED**

3. Working one at a time, set one square of paper in the bottom of the press and place a dough ball in the center. Top with another square of paper and press down until the dough flattens into a thin tortilla. You want it to look and feel as thin as your favorite store-bought tortillas. To roll these out with a rolling pin, place the dough ball between the two pieces of paper and roll until the dough is as flat as a store-bought tortilla. Don't sweat it if you can't roll them into perfect circles; they'll taste great no matter the shape.

4. Carefully peel back the top layer of paper to reveal the tortilla underneath. Pick up the bottom sheet of paper that has the flattened tortilla attached to it. Carefully flip it on the hot cast-iron skillet (with paper facing up) and let it heat up with the paper attached for about 10 seconds. Peel off the paper to make sure the tortilla comes off evenly without breaking. You can also use a slotted fish spatula, but I found this method to be a bit simpler.

5. Flip the tortilla once it starts to bubble up, after about 1 minute. Flip a couple of times until cooked through. Place the tortilla in a holder or between two tea towels to keep it warm before serving. These are best eaten on the same day.

# COCONUT TORTILLA CHIPS

**SERVES 8 TO 10 • PREPARATION TIME 15 MINUTES**

These are different from your average store-bought chips because they don't have a ton of ingredients and won't last as long on the shelf. Made with my Coconut Tortillas with Lard, they are also gluten-, grain-, and nut-free. Trust me, you won't find anything like these at the grocery store. Plus, it's a great way to use up your homemade tortillas if they are going stale. I like to fry these in oil and salt them straight out of the pan. If you prefer a baked version with less oil, I've included that as well.

2 to 3 cups avocado oil for frying

10 Coconut Tortillas with Lard (page 209), cut into triangles

Kosher salt

*To make the fried version*: Pour the oil into a cast-iron skillet or a heavy pan with some depth. Make sure the oil is at least 1 inch deep in the pan. Line a baking sheet with paper towels. Heat the oil to a medium-high heat until it sizzles when you dip in the corner of a tortilla. Using a slotted spoon or tongs, place the cut triangles into the oil for about 2 minutes, until they reach a golden brown color, flipping halfway through. I like to fry these in batches, making sure not to crowd the pan. Remove the chips as they turn golden brown, shaking off the extra oil. Place the fried chips on the prepared sheet to absorb excess oil, and salt them while hot. Continue this method, working in batches.

*To make the baked version*: Preheat the oven to 350°F. Brush or spray the oil onto the tortillas. Coat them carefully so they crisp up in the oven. Place the tortillas in an even layer on a large baking sheet and sprinkle them with salt. Make sure they are not overlapping or crowded on the sheet. Bake for 10 to 12 minutes, until golden brown. They will continue to crisp as they cool.

These chips store well for a couple of days in an airtight container at room temperature.

# HANDMADE CORN TORTILLAS

2 cups masa harina

½ teaspoon sea salt

1½ to 2 cups hot water

**MAKES 12 TORTILLAS • PREPARATION TIME 30 MINUTES, PLUS 1 HOUR RESTING**

Unfortunately, corn (*maize*) has very little nutritional value. It's high in lectins and sugar, can contain mold, and can be very inflammatory. Maize is more of a cultural staple to Mexican cooking and is a vessel for most of the recipes we know and love today. The corn they used years ago is not the same as the corn we use today. About 90 percent of the corn grown in the United States is genetically modified. It also contains prolamins, which are a class of proteins that our bodies cannot break down efficiently, leading to or affecting gut issues, like leaky gut, and negatively impacting the growth of bad bacteria in your gut.

Out with the old gross store-bought tortillas. Most tortillas you buy in the store—yes, even the ones with all of the "healthy corn" teasers on the label—contain most of the following: cellulose gum, phosphoric acid, propionic acid, guar gum, added enzymes, sorbic acid, calcium sulfide, benzoic acid, canola and other vegetables oils, and fumaric acid. That is quite different from your three-ingredient homemade ones.

---

### CORN HISTORY

Making your own *masa* is a very intensive process and dates back to the Aztecs in 1200 BCE.

The traditional tortilla is made by curing maize in limewater to make it usable, an ancient process called *nixtamalization*. This allows the skin of the corn kernels to gently peel off. The maize then becomes workable and can be shaped into a ground dough.

1. In a medium bowl, mix together the masa harina and salt. Slowly pour in the hot water and mix with your hands until the dough is firm and springy, not dry or sticky, when touched. Let rest for about an hour. I like to cover mine with a damp kitchen towel.

2. Once the dough is rested, use your hands to break off pieces and roll into twelve 2-inch balls. If using your tortilla press, cut two pieces of waxed paper or parchment paper. Place the rolled balls in the middle of the paper and press or roll out if using a rolling pin.

3. Preheat a *comal*, cast-iron skillet, or flat cooking surface of choice to medium-high heat. Cook each pressed tortilla for about 1 minute on each side. Once the tortilla is golden brown, wrap the cooked tortillas in a towel to keep warm and serve immediately. They will last 4 to 5 days in the fridge, or you can freeze them for a few weeks.

**TORIE'S TORTILLA TIPS (SAY THAT THREE TIMES FAST!)**

Do not try to rush this process.

Do not try making tortillas for the first time when having guests.

USDA organic will always be a non-GMO product, so always choose organic.

Try adding spices and herbs for color and an extra nutritional boost. I like chia, turmeric, and chiles.

# GOAT CHEESE QUESADILLAS WITH HIBISCUS AND SEASONAL VEGGIES

**SERVES 4 • PREPARATION TIME 10 MINUTES**

Who doesn't love a quesadilla? I created this delicious fancy version one day with some leftover hibiscus flowers from my tea. Yummy! The hibiscus adds texture and a slight tang while the goat cheese adds creaminess, making for a very grown-up spin on a childhood favorite. I added summer squash because they were in season at the time, but feel free to add your own twist, like mushrooms, salsa fresca, or sautéed greens. Serve with my Habanero Pepita "Cheese" Salsa (page 67) or Probiotic Guacamole (page 91).

3 cups water

½ cup dried hibiscus flowers

1 tablespoon MCT oil, avocado oil, or pasture-raised lard

1 tablespoon coconut oil

1 yellow or green summer squash, diced small

Coconut or avocado oil for spraying

4 Coconut Tortillas with Lard (page 209) or your favorite tortillas

¼ cup goat cheese

1. In a large saucepan, bring the water to a low boil and add the hibiscus flowers. Turn off the heat and let steep for 5 minutes. Drain the hibiscus using a strainer and save the liquid to make an iced tea for later. (I like to put the flowers in ice cube trays for my next fiesta.) Toss the hydrated hibiscus flowers with MCT oil for that extra healthy fat!

2. In a small pan on medium heat, melt the coconut oil. Add the diced squash and sauté until soft and slightly fragrant, about 5 minutes. Set aside.

3. In a cast-iron skillet over medium heat, spray a little coconut oil or avocado oil and add your first tortilla. Sprinkle half of the cheese, hibiscus flowers, and squash on top, and cover with another tortilla (or you can fill with one-fourth of ingredients and fold in half as pictured). Heat for about 3 minutes so the cheese starts to soften. Using a spatula or tongs, flip it over and let it cook another few minutes. Place on the cutting board and cut into slices if desired. Repeat with the remaining ingredients. Serve immediately.

# "REFRIED" BEANS, BONES, AND EPAZOTE

1 pound dried black or pinto beans

¼ teaspoon baking soda and/or 1 piece dried kombu

1 to 2 marrow bones

1 white onion, roughly chopped

2 to 4 garlic cloves

1 teaspoon kosher salt

1 tablespoon dried epazote or oregano

1 teaspoon chili powder

1 teaspoon ground cumin

2 to 3 chipotles in adobo sauce, minced

2 to 3 tablespoons avocado oil

2 cups Healing Mexican Bone Broth (page 120; optional)

Chopped cilantro, sliced limes, and fresh cheese for topping

**SERVES 8 • PREPARATION TIME 2 HOURS, PLUS OVERNIGHT SOAKING**

Beans are high in carbs so they are not very keto, but I couldn't write a Mexican cookbook without a *frijole* recipe. Beans are from the legume family, and people with digestive problems should stay away from them. A cook at our hotel in Baja makes these refried beans with bone marrow, and I can never resist them. And for some reason, they never hurt my stomach.

I like to add ¼ teaspoon of baking soda to help break down and tenderize beans. Add a piece of kombu to help with digestion. Keep in mind that soaking beans beforehand may also cut down on cooking times. Limes served with certain foods—in this case beans—have been shown to help with the absorption of iron.

1. Soak the beans overnight in cool water with the baking soda and/or kombu. The water should cover the beans by at least 2 inches. Drain the soaked beans in a colander and rinse really well (this liquid is where the gassy compounds are now). Transfer the soaked and rinsed beans to a stockpot and add the bones, onion, garlic, salt, epazote, chili powder, cumin, chipotles, and avocado oil.

2. Cover the beans and bones with cold filtered water or a mix of bone broth (if using) and water. The bones should be covered by ½ to 1 inch of liquid. Bring to a boil, skimming and discarding any foam that rises to the top. Leave the mixture uncovered on a low boil for 20 minutes, allowing the steam to rise. This breaks up and disperses the indigestible enzymes.

3. Lower the heat to a simmer and simmer, covered, for 1 to 2 hours, until the beans are soft and the marrow is opaque and cooked through. Check on the beans 50 minutes into cooking for texture and flavor, adding more seasoning if needed.

4. When the beans are soft and the marrow is cooked through, use tongs and a butter knife to slip the soft marrow out of the center of the bones. Discard the actual bones or reserve them for another use (like broth). You can leave the beans as they are (semi-whole) in the broth or roughly smash them or use an immersion blender to make them more of a refried style. Serve with cilantro, limes, fresh cheese, or your favorite toppings.

# MEXICAN RED RICE WITH BUTTER AND TOMATOES

**SERVES 8 TO 10 • PREPARATION TIME 50 MINUTES**

This classic tomato-and-butter–based rice is a staple in most Mexican kitchens. You'll find it on the plate next to your refried beans anywhere from the Mexican restaurant on the corner to Grandma's table in Baja or the mainland. Remember, white rice is better for you than brown rice, if you are dealing with an inflammatory issue, I highly suggest substituting this with my cauliflower version (see page 134).

---

1. Place the tomatoes, garlic, onion, ½ teaspoon salt, and cumin in a blender or food processor and puree until smooth. Set aside.

2. In a heavy pan, heat the butter on medium heat and add the rice. Sauté the rice in the fat for 5 to 7 minutes, until lightly toasted and golden brown. Add the minced chiles and cook until they have softened, about 2 minutes.

3. Pour the pureed tomato mixture over the rice and stir to combine, scraping the bottom of the pan. Cook on low to medium heat until the mixture has been absorbed, 5 to 7 minutes, then add the stock. Turn the heat to low, cover, and cook until the liquid has evaporated and the rice is tender, about 20 minutes.

4. Remove the rice from the heat and gently stir in the lime juice and more salt if desired. Re-cover the rice and allow it to rest, undisturbed, for an additional 10 minutes. Fluff with a fork and serve with lime wedges.

2 cups canned whole or stewed peeled tomatoes

2 garlic cloves, minced

¼ cup finely chopped white onion

Kosher salt

½ teaspoon ground cumin

⅓ cup grass-fed butter, ghee, pasture-raised lard, coconut oil, or MCT oil

1½ cups uncooked long-grain white rice

1 to 2 serrano or jalapeño chiles, seeds removed, minced

2 cups Classic Chicken Stock (page 121) or Healing Mexican Bone Broth (page 120)

Juice of 2 limes

Lime wedges, for serving

# LOW-CARB RICE

2 cups canned whole or stewed peeled tomatoes

2 garlic cloves, minced

¼ cup finely chopped white onion

1 teaspoon sea salt

½ teaspoon ground cumin

4 tablespoons grass-fed butter, ghee, pasture-raised lard, coconut oil, or MCT oil

3 cups cooked (with coconut oil) and cooled long-grain white rice

1 to 2 serrano chiles, seeds removed, minced

1 cup Classic Chicken Stock (page 121) or Healing Mexican Bone Broth (page 120)

Juice of 2 limes

Lime wedges, for serving

**SERVES 4 TO 6 • PREPARATION TIME 30 MINUTES**

Rice is something I think people tend to stay away from on a strict keto diet. I have found that if you add coconut oil to the cooking process (see facing page) and then cool rice before consuming it, you change how your body absorbs the carbohydrate. This lowers the glycemic response in the body and therefore keeps your glucose (blood sugar) level from spiking—a reason people gain weight.

For me and most of my women clients who focus on a HFLC (high-fat, low-carb) diet, eating the right carbs helps to maintain energy level and hormone balance. There is a time and place for a more strict keto (when you have a serious disease), but I definitely feel better when I get my serving of those good carbs, and I like to do it at nighttime. I am *not* telling you to eat rice every day, but I am saying that you should listen to your body; and when you eat white rice, add your fat (MCT oil, coconut oil, or butter), cool it, and enjoy.

1. Place the canned tomatoes, garlic, onion, salt, and cumin in a blender or food processor and puree until smooth. Set aside.

2. In a heavy pan, heat the butter over medium heat and add the cooked rice. Sauté the rice in the fat for 3 to 5 minutes, until lightly toasted and golden brown. Add the minced chiles and cook until they have softened, about 2 minutes.

3. Pour the pureed tomato mixture over the rice and stir to combine, scraping the bottom of the pan. Once the tomato mixture has been absorbed, add the stock. Turn the heat to low, cover, and cook until the liquid has evaporated and the rice is tender, 5 to 7 minutes.

4. Remove the rice from the heat and gently stir in the lime juice and more salt if desired. Re-cover the rice and allow it to rest, undisturbed, for an additional 10 minutes. Fluff with a fork and serve with lime wedges.

## TIPS TO COOK LOW-CARB RICE

There are two main ideas to keep in mind when making low-carb rice.

1. Cook and cool your rice. Research shows that cooking and then cooling your rice creates higher-resistant starch. It reduces how we are absorbing those carbs (starch content), giving us less of a sugar (glucose) spike.

2. Cook the rice with a form of coconut oil. Basically, add a spoonful or two of your favorite coconut oil to rice and make it as you normally would, allowing it to cool completely before eating or reheating.

### BROWN RICE VERSUS WHITE RICE

Get ready, because I am about to burst your bubble. Brown rice is not healthier than white rice. Yeah, you and everyone else are shocked, I know. Basically, brown rice contains arsenic; levels can vary based on the variety and country of origin. Brown rice also has a compound called phytic acid, which makes it more difficult to digest.

# BUTTERNUT SQUASH-GOAT CHEESE ENCHILADAS WITH TOMATILLO SALSA

1 large butternut squash, peeled, seeded, and diced into small 1-inch cubes (about 5 cups)

4 tablespoons MCT oil or avocado oil

1 teaspoon chili powder

1 teaspoon turmeric powder

1 teaspoon kosher salt

1 small yellow or white onion, chopped (about 2 cups)

½ teaspoon freshly ground black pepper

3 cups mushrooms (shiitake, portobello, hen of the woods, chanterelle, or oyster), roughly chopped

11 to 15 ounces softened goat cheese

3 cups Green Tomatillo Salsa (page 63)

12 tortillas (see pages 209 and 214)

**TOPPINGS**

Fresh cilantro, cheese, green onions, thinly sliced avocado, Vegan Cashew Spread (page 72), or Baja Crema with Lime (page 70)

**SERVES 8 TO 10 • PREPARATION TIME 1 HOUR**

The filling of this recipe can be made up to three days in advance and is also great to keep in the freezer for a quick weekday meal or dinner party. The sauce can also be made in advance and refrigerated.

Deep-orange butternut squash flesh is full of fiber, beta-carotene, and vitamins A and C, and it has a naturally sweet flavor that really emerges when roasted. This recipe is naturally vegetarian and can easily be made vegan by removing the small amount of goat cheese. You can also use a dairy-free option.

If you want to make these enchiladas in summer, you can substitute a mixture of the season's best peppers or your favorite seasonal squash variety. If you want to add protein, shred an organic rotisserie chicken on top.

---

1. To make the filling: Preheat the oven to 400°F.

2. In a large bowl, toss the squash cubes with 2 tablespoons of the oil, the chili powder, turmeric, and salt. Transfer the cubes to a rimmed baking sheet and arrange so they are not touching each other. Place the baking sheet into the oven and roast the squash for 15 to 18 minutes, until tender and lightly browned. Remove from the oven and set aside. Lower the oven temperature to 350°F.

3. While the squash is baking, add the remaining 2 tablespoons of oil to a sauté pan over medium heat and sauté the onion, black pepper, and mushrooms for 8 to 10 minutes, stirring often, until the onion is translucent and both the onion and mushrooms have softened. Remove the sautéed vegetables from the pan and transfer them to a large bowl.

4. Add the roasted butternut squash to the bowl and mix in half of the goat cheese. Mix until the ingredients are evenly combined.

5. Spread about ¾ cup of the tomatillo salsa in a thin layer on the bottom of an 11 by 13-inch baking dish. Warm your tortillas on a *comal* or cast-iron, flipping once to soften.

6. Working one tortilla at a time on a clean, flat surface, place about 2 tablespoons of the squash mixture to one side of each tortilla. Then roll the tortilla up like a burrito and place it in the baking dish with the seam-side down. Keep an eye on how much filling you use so that you can roll the enchiladas shut and to make sure you have enough to fill eleven more. Repeat until you have stuffed all of the tortillas.

7. Spoon the remaining tomatillo salsa over the enchiladas and top with the remaining goat cheese. Place the baking dish on the middle rack of the oven and bake for 30 minutes, until the cheese is golden brown and everything is bubbling.

8. Remove the finished enchiladas from the oven and let cool for 5 minutes before topping with a sprinkle of fresh cilantro. Serve your enchiladas with more cheese, green onions, thinly sliced avocado, or top with my Vegan Cashew Spread or Baja Crema with Lime.

# MUSHROOM VEGETARIAN TOSTADA WITH ALL THE TOPPINGS

## MUSHROOM SPREAD

2 tablespoons ghee or avocado oil

1 cup chopped shallots or white onion

Kosher salt

4 to 5 cups mixed mushrooms (cremini, porcini, shiitake, oyster, or chanterelle), chopped small

2 garlic cloves, roughly chopped

1 teaspoon apple cider vinegar

2 tablespoons MCT oil

1 teaspoon freshly ground black pepper

## TOSTADAS

Avocado oil or avocado oil spray

10 tortillas (see pages 209 and 214)

## TOPPINGS

Baja Crema with Lime (page 70), shredded lettuce, One-Day Pickled Slaw (page 101), Salsa Bandera (page 62), Probiotic Guacamole (page 91), cotija or feta, pickled or fermented vegetables (see page 141)

**SERVES 8 TO 10 • PREPARATION TIME 30 MINUTES**

The base of this recipe is a mixed mushroom spread that gives the sensation and heartiness of beans but without the carbs. You can always find porcini or shiitake mushrooms in the dried section of the market; they are great pantry staples. Just add hot water and—*boom*—you have elevated your dish and added mouthwatering umami flavor.

I love how mushrooms have taken off in the health world. From lion's mane to micro-dosing, mushrooms are great to take in a supplement and on your plate. There's a lot of exciting work exploring the therapeutic properties of psychedelics. You can read more about adaptogens on page 30.

This mushroom spread would also be good in Mexican Crudité (page 80) as a pâté or dip. The tostadas can be baked in the oven or shallow-fried.

1. In a saucepan or cast-iron skillet over medium-low heat, combine the ghee, shallots, and a pinch of salt. Sauté for 5 to 8 minutes, until the shallots are translucent and the edges begin to caramelize. Add the mushrooms, garlic, and vinegar and sauté for about 20 minutes until the mushrooms soften and are cooked through. Remove the pan from the heat and put the ingredients into a food processor or blender and blend until smooth. You can make the spread a few days ahead and store in the fridge.

2. *To bake the tostadas*: Preheat the oven to 450°F. Spray avocado oil on both sides of each tortilla (or brush them slightly if you do not have spray). Place them lightly touching each other on a baking sheet. Bake for 15 minutes, until crispy, flipping halfway through or rotating the pans, depending on your oven.

   *To shallow-fry the tostadas*: Line a baking sheet with paper towels. Pour the avocado oil into the cast-iron skillet or a small pan, making sure the oil comes about 1 inch up the side of the pan. Heat the skillet and oil to medium heat. Using a slotted spoon or tongs, place one tortilla into the oil for about 2 minutes, until it reaches a golden brown color. Do the tortillas one by one so as not to crowd the pan. Remove each one as it turns golden, and shake off the extra oil. Place on the prepared baking sheet to absorb excess oil and then season with salt. Continue until all the tostadas are fried.

3. Top the tortillas with the mushroom spread and desired toppings and serve immediately.

NOTE If using dried mushrooms, place them in a bowl and pour boiling water over them to cover. Let soak about 30 minutes. Do not discard the precious juice; save it and add it to your broths or use it instead of chicken broth to cook veggies.

# ACKNOWLEDGMENTS

Muchas gracias to all of the Mexicans behind every restaurant. I am honored by the passion and community that binds us, which in the end has inspired me to write this book. You are willing to work the hardest, learn and grow, and most of all, feed anyone and everyone until they are *relleno* ("stuffed"). This book is for everyone, but so much for the people suffering in Mexico who love food, but are confused on what to eat. Keep learning and digging deep and remember what abuela ate. *Buen Provecho!*

My loving, supportive, and Mexican abuela, Dora, who has been my number-one fan and a huge support in making this cookbook possible. The health issues you've faced after shifting from a traditional Mexican diet to the American way of eating and the suffering it has caused you is a perfect example of why the world needs this book. I'm grateful we can work hard together to fill your fridge with all the foods you knew and loved in your younger life, many of which are in this book.

My husband, Josh, who makes every day better. Thank you for your willingness to sample my experiments in the kitchen and to partake in all of my food diets, fasts, lab work, finger pricks, and ketone tests. I know you love receiving the constant compliments on how good you look because of this lifestyle. You keep me from getting lost in the craziness and self pressure of my work, and you help me feel grounded. Thank you for your frequent reminders to take a step back, rethink my reactions, and instead be grateful. Your encouragement to always go catch at least one wave has me coming out of the water feeling better and more clear headed. Without your endless support and love I wouldn't have been able to even sign a book deal or make my dreams become this reality.

My parents who tested so many recipes, and who are always boosting me up to their friends. I feel so blessed to have you as my mentors. I love you more than you will ever know.

My sister Allie who comes over just in time to eat my food most days of the week. You inspire me to keep organized and you're always here to clean up my kitchen mess. Without your leadership for our team at the hotel, my ideas wouldn't have penetrated the town.

My youngest sister, Bettina, is always open to hearing my new ideas and spreading the knowledge to others. Thank you for learning from me and for your excitement to try anything from cleanses to weird recipe ideas. Your enthusiasm for alternative healing and a balanced body (inside and out) adds another angle to what I do.

My cousin Kylee who always seems to find time to help me in everything from cooking to editing. Your input and time spent helping allowed me to make some critical decisions on this and all my projects.

My Italian abuelo, Pop. Who is no longer with us but with me in everything I do that revolves around culture and food. You were a proud Italian who fell in love with Mexico; in part because the Mexican side of the family gave you no choice and a lot because you felt a connection with the people and the culture in the same way I do. You always got by just fine in Mexico with Italian and a couple tequilas.

My Scorpion Bay *familia* who endlessly listen to my nutrition classes and new recipes with no judgment. I have seen incredible results from our staff and community even with limited resources (no electricity). I'm amazed by your ability to make changes in your lives and learn new things.

Nicole, my editor, who listened to what I was saying and looked at what I wrote and helped me say it way better by simplifying my science-forward thinking. You have been on my side when this was just a mere idea and never laughed (too loud) at my oh so many questions.

Rancho La Puerta for allowing me to be a part of your family, your team, and the special home you are to so many. Since a young age, I've felt so inspired and creative when at the Ranch, teaching or working with guests and local staff. Thank you for sharing this journey with me.

The most incredible photographer, Eric. From Day One (about 3 years ago), you had my back. You saw my vision and literally made it a reality. You never gave up on me, *muchas pinche gracias*. Thank goodness for you getting me, and for your continual reminders that this book will come to life and just to be patient. Thank you for your enthusiasm of trying out keto and intermittent fasting, and being a pretty great student at that. We did it and we are going to help so many people.

Amigos, familia, and strangers who all volunteered to be recipe testers (you know who you are), you have been there to give me honest feedback and to help these recipes become what they are. I am forever grateful.

Thank you to the many doctors who have shaped me and educated me in my journey.

Thanks to the team at Ten Speed Press. There is SO much that goes on in creating a cookbook and I will be forever grateful for the support.

Dervla Kelly who supported me throughout the entire process and also edited the entire thing.

Designer: Lizzie Allen with design and vision.

Senior art director: Emma Campion

Production: Serena Sigona

PR and Marketing: Kristin Casemore and Eleanor Thacher

# ABOUT THE AUTHOR

TORIE BORRELLI is an integrative holistic nutritionist, wellness consultant, recipe creator, and founder of The Vida Well, a brand rooted in nutrition education and wholesome living. Her Mexican and Italian heritage birthed a lifelong love of food, but personal health issues were ultimately the impetus behind Torie's pursuit of an education in holistic medicine and nutritional cooking. Borrelli is an instructor at Rancho La Puerta Wellness Resort and Spa in Tecate, Mexico, and a collaborator with brands such as ButcherBox, Bulletproof, Siete Family Foods, Lyft, Kopari Beauty, and Coola Suncare.

# INDEX

Text copyright © 2019 by Torie Borelli.
Photographs copyright © 2019 by Eric Wolfinger, with the exception of
pages 14–15, 21, and 28 by Lucianna McIntosh.

All rights reserved.

Published in the United States by Ten Speed Press, an imprint of
Random House, a division of Penguin Random House LLC, New York.
www.tenspeed.com

Ten Speed Press and the Ten Speed Press colophon are registered
trademarks of Penguin Random House LLC.

Library of Congress Cataloging-in-Publication Data
    Names: Borrelli, Torie, 1987- author.
    Title: The Mexican Keto cookbook / Torie Borrelli.
    Description: First edition. | California : Ten Speed Press, 2019. |
    Includes index.
    Identifiers: LCCN 2019014746 | ISBN 9781984857088 (hardcover)
    Subjects: LCSH: Cooking–New Mexico. | LCGFT: Cookbooks.
    Classification: LCC TX716.M4 B66 2019 | DDC 641.50972–dc23 LC
    record available at https://lccn.loc.gov/2019014746

Hardcover ISBN: 978-1-9848-5708-8
eBook ISBN: 978-1-9848-5709-5

Printed in China

Design by Lizzie Allen

10 9 8 7 6 5 4 3 2 1

First Edition